Yitzhak Rabin

YITZHAK RABIN

ISRAEL'S SOLDIER STATESMAN

MICHAEL G. KORT

The Millbrook Press
Brookfield, Connecticut

Library of Congress Cataloging-in-Publication Data
Kort, Michael, 1944–
Yitzhak Rabin: Israel's soldier statesman / by Michael G. Kort.
p. cm.
Includes bibliographical references and index.
ISBN 0-7613-0100-3 (lib. bdg.) ISBN 0-7613-0135-6 (tr. pbk.)
1. Rabin, Yitzhak, 1922–1995–Juvenile literature. 2. Prime ministers–
Israel–Biography–Juvenile literature. 3. Generals–Israel–Biography–
Juvenile literature. 4. Israel–History–Juvenile literature. I. Title.
DS126.6.R32K67 1996
956.9405'092–dc20 [B] 96–17595 CIP AC

Photographs courtesy and © Israel Government Press Office: pp. 24, 29,
50, 73; UPI/Corbis-Bettmann: pp. 37, 39, 45, 52, 76, 83, 86, 105, 111,
159; Wide World: pp. 69, 145, 161; Ruben Bittermann, Impact Visuals: pp.
137, 157; map by Frank Senyk.

Published by The Millbrook Press
2 Old New Milford Road, Brookfield, Connecticut 06804

*For my uncles, Heini and Max
and their children, grandchildren,
and great-grandchildren,
in Israel.*

I would like to thank Zvi Meth of Haifa, Israel, for his invaluable help in locating materials I needed for this book. I am very grateful to Norman H. Finkelstein and Lawrence Lowenthall, who read and critiqued the entire manuscript, and to Paula Fredriksen and Richard Landes, who read and discussed with me at length several sections of the manuscript that dealt with particularly difficult issues. My wife, Carol, deserves a special thanks, not just for editing the manuscript, as she always does so well, but for coming up with the idea for this book and then insisting that I write it.

Michael G. Kort

CONTENTS

Yitzhak Rabin

JERUSALEM

0   5 Miles
0   5 Kilometers

ISRAEL

WEST
BANK

Old City

West
Jerusalem
1949-67

Jewish
Quarter

1949 armistice line

No Man's Land 1949-67

LEBANON

SYRIA

GOLAN
HEIGHTS
(annexed by
Israel 1981)

Kiryat
Shemona

Sea of Galilee
(Israeli name:
Lake Kinneret)

Haifa

ISRAEL

Jordan
River

Mediterranean Sea

Tel Aviv

Jerusalem

WEST BANK

GAZA STRIP

Dead Sea

Beersheba

Suez
Canal

NEGEV
DESERT

JORDAN

SINAI
PENINSULA

Elat

Gulf of
Aqaba
(Israeli name:
Gulf of Elat)

SAUDI

Gulf of Suez

0   50   100 Miles
0   50   100 Kilometers

EGYPT

Strait of Tiran

ARABIA

Red Sea

CHAPTER ONE

"The hopes of the Jewish people."

October 10, 1945, was a moonless night along the coast of the Mediterranean Sea in British-controlled Palestine. Eight miles (13 kilometers) south of the city of Haifa, 203 Jewish prisoners waited inside a makeshift detention camp called Atlit. The well lit camp glowed against the surrounding darkness. The mood inside the camp's barbed-wire fences and barracks mirrored the stark contrast outside. There was despair as dark as the enveloping night as the prisoners awaited their fate at the hands of the British. Yet hope also glowed because the prisoners knew the Jewish community of Palestine had not abandoned them.

The Jews in the Atlit camp were not criminals. They were refugees, survivors of the Holocaust, whose murderous fires finally had been extinguished by the Allied victory over Nazi Germany only months before. The refugees in Atlit had left Europe and entered Palestine during 1945 by sneaking across the border from Syria on foot. This made them "illegal" immigrants according to the British, who controlled Palestine. British policy was to put strict limits on Jewish immigration into Palestine to avoid antagonizing the Arab population of the region. Jews who slipped into the country illegally and were caught were deported. Meanwhile, 250,000 Jewish survivors of the Holocaust in Europe wandered from place to place or waited in crowded and filthy detention camps with no place in the world to go.

The Jewish community of Palestine, which numbered about 650,000, was resisting British immigration policy. That is why on this night in October more than 200 Jewish soldiers waited in darkness about 100 yards (914 meters) outside the camp. These soldiers did not belong to a regular army. They were members of the Palmach, the elite military unit of the Hagana, the self-defense organization of Palestine's Jewish community. The Palmach's main job was to protect the Jewish population against increasingly serious attacks from local Arabs. At the same time it tried to help Jewish refugees from Europe avoid British authorities and get into Palestine.

The Palmach's task on October 10 was to free the refugees from the Atlit camp and hide them among the general population. Its troops outside the camp were divided into three groups. One group would wait outside to set up roadblocks and fight any British troops who tried to interfere with the planned operation. A second group prepared to take the refugees to nearby trucks after they were freed from the camp. They would then be driven to a Jewish agricultural settlement called Kibbutz Yagur. The third group had the job of breaking into the camp and getting the prisoners out beyond the fences. It was led by the second-in-command of the overall operation, a handsome twenty-three-year-old with a reputation for quick thinking and staying calm under fire. His name was Yitzhak Rabin.

Rabin was worried, less about his tough soldiers who were risking their lives than about the desperate people they were trying to liberate. He was thinking: "These people were survivors of the Holocaust, the few snatched from the conflagration. We would never forgive ourselves if any harm were to befall them."[1]

Inside Atlit the escape was carefully prepared. The Palmach had sent agents into the camp posing as teachers. They organized the refugees for the breakout. The "teachers" also secretly disabled the rifles of Arabs employed by the British to help guard the camp.

The job of getting the refugees out of the camp went quickly and smoothly. Rabin's men cut their way through the fence wires and entered the camp. They immediately met some "teachers" who told Rabin they had broken the firing pins on the rifles of the Arab guards. Thanks to their efforts, when Rabin and his men ran into the Arab guards, they "cocked their guns, pressed the triggers, and nothing happened." It also was very helpful, Rabin remembered later, that the British at the camp "were fast asleep."[2]

It took barely 30 minutes to get the refugees out of the camp. Then the trouble began. The men, women, and children freed from the camp refused to leave behind their few bundles and suitcases, as Rabin recalled, "the only possessions they had left."[3] Meanwhile, they could not help dropping bits and pieces of their possessions as they marched, leaving a perfect trail for British spotter planes that would soon be searching for them to follow. Making matters worse, infants, small children, and the weaker adults slowed up the group.

Rabin quickly conferred with the operation's overall commander, a veteran soldier named Nahum Sarig. Rabin and Sarig knew the entire group could never reach the waiting trucks before the British arrived. They decided to split the refugees. Sarig would take the stronger refugees, who could move fastest, to the waiting trucks and on to Kibbutz Yagur. Rabin with about 60 troops would look after the rest of the group. He would march them on foot to a nearer Jewish settlement, Kibbutz Bet Oren.

A difficult journey lay ahead of Rabin and the 100 Holocaust survivors "whose fate was now in my hands."[4] To reach Bet Oren, Rabin's group had to climb up a ridge about 1,800 feet (550 meters) high known as Mount Carmel, which extends about 15 miles (24 kilometers) along the Mediterranean shore. The Bible records that in ancient times the Israelite prophet Elijah performed miracles there. Rabin performed no miracles that October night, or the next day, but he must have seemed like a miracle worker to the terrified children and weakened adults under his care.

The climb up rugged Mount Carmel went far more slowly than planned. Rabin's soldiers had to carry the children on their shoulders. As Rabin carried one of them he thought of how "my shoulders bore the hopes of the Jewish people." Those shoulders also bore a child "paralyzed with fear." Rabin soon had evidence of how afraid the child was when he "suddenly felt a warm, damp sensation running down my back. Under the circumstances, I could hardly halt."[5]

During the march to Bet Oren a British patrol in a truck ran across Rabin's group. In the shooting that followed, a British sergeant was killed, the only casualty of the Atlit operation.

Sarig's group reached Kibbutz Yagur before dawn, and the refugees were scattered among the residents. Things went less smoothly for Rabin's weary troop. By the time it reached Bet Oren, it was daylight. British soldiers surrounded the settlement. Rabin hid his people in the woods outside the settlement and sent scouts to see if a way could be found through the encirclement. They found a gap in the British lines. Rabin quickly moved his people into the kibbutz. The refugees immediately were placed in different homes while Rabin and his men hid their weapons, which they carried illegally.

As these tasks were being completed, the British realized what had happened, and it seemed as if they would force their way into the settlement and carry off the refugees. Help arrived just in time from the nearby city of Haifa. The Hagana organized 15,000 people to get on buses and come to Bet Oren. As the British watched, unwilling to shoot unarmed Jewish civilians who were committing no crime, thousands of people poured into Bet Oren. Rabin remembered: "By afternoon the whole area was teeming with people, and the immigrants were swallowed up by a human sea. The British conceded defeat."[6]

Word quickly spread of the Atlit operation and Rabin's role in it. His girlfriend, Leah Schlossberg, who later became his wife, remembers how she was congratulated because of Yitzhak's success. As for Rabin, always a man of few words, he only said, "The planning and the execution weren't bad."[7]

CHAPTER TWO

"All right. You'll do."

I n his memoirs, Yitzhak Rabin wondered about how his parents came to meet and set the stage for his own life:

> *Some marriages, I am told, are made in heaven. I cannot testify that some otherworldly force guided my parents toward their first meeting. But the crossing of their paths was such an unlikely event that it's almost a wonder that I am here to relate the subsequent story of my life.[1]*

Actually, what brought Rabin's parents together was Zionism. This movement was founded on the belief that Jews should return from the countries in which they lived all over the world and rebuild their ancient homeland in the land of Israel. The movement is as old as the disasters that befell the Jews almost 2,000 years ago, when the Romans crushed Jewish independence revolts in A.D. 70 and 135, destroyed the city of Jerusalem, and drove most Jews from the country where they had been living for more than 1,500 years. At the time of the rebellions against Rome, the country was called Judea. After the second Jewish revolt, the conquering Romans tried to cut the link between the Jews and their homeland by changing its name to Palestine.

That link, however, was never broken, regardless of whether the Romans, Byzantines, Persians, Arabs, Crusaders, Mamelukes, Turks, or British ruled in Palestine. Although Jews became a minority in Palestine, Jewish communities in Jerusalem and cities like Safed, Tiberias, and Hebron, as well as in other parts of the country, continued to exist and recover after periods of disaster and persecution. In their communities throughout the world outside Palestine, which the Jews called the Diaspora, they prayed to return to Jerusalem and the land of their ancestors. Zionism remained a belief rather than an organized movement until the late nineteenth century. Then, faced with growing anti-Semitism in Europe, Jews who believed in Zionism began to organize. By the 1880s the first large groups of Jews from Europe began returning to Palestine. They joined the old communities of Jews that throughout the centuries had lived in Jerusalem and other parts of the country. The new arrivals from Europe in turn were joined by several thousand Jews escaping Muslim persecution in Yemen, a country located on the Arabian Peninsula.

At that time Palestine was part of the Ottoman, or Turkish, Empire, which had conquered the territory in 1517. The Turks were Muslims, as were the Arabs who were the majority of Palestine's population.

Palestine was extremely poor and barren and thinly settled. In the 1880s the total Arab population in all of Palestine west of the Jordan River (which includes today's Israel *and* the West Bank and Gaza Strip) was about 250,000. Most Arabs were peasant farmers who lived in small isolated villages. Jews were the majority in Jerusalem, in those days a neglected and poverty-stricken city of less than 30,000 people, as well as in Tiberias and Safed. Wherever they lived in Palestine, Jews faced constant discrimination and periodic violence at the hands of the Muslim Arab majority.

The Jews who were returning to Palestine did not intend to displace the local Arabs. They were convinced that their efforts to rebuild the country would enable it to support all the people living there, both Arabs and Jews. In fact, as Jewish immigrants from Europe developed the local economy, many Arabs from surrounding territories immigrated into Palestine. After 1880 the population of Palestine, both Arab and Jewish, grew rapidly, both as a result of immigration and improved local health conditions. By 1914, Palestine west of the Jordan River had a population of about 650,000, about 85,000 of whom were Jews. However, the Arabs feared that Jews would eventually become a majority in Palestine and win control of the country. This they were unwilling to accept. The Arabs considered the Jews arriving from Europe to be intruders, and as early as the 1880s they began to oppose Jewish immigration.

Zionism took various forms. While some Zionists were deeply religious, most were not. Many Zionists were influenced by socialist ideas. They wanted to build a new Jewish society in Palestine based on the socialist principles of cooperation and equality. Both Nehemiah

Robichov, who was born in Russia in 1886 and who in 1917 changed his last name to Rabin, and Rosa Cohen, who was born in Russia in 1890, belonged to the socialist wing of the Zionist movement. Nehemiah and Rosa would become Yitzhak Rabin's father and mother.

Nehemiah Robichov was born in a poor village near Kiev, today the capital of Ukraine but in those days part of the huge Russian Empire. He started working when he was ten and left home at fourteen. At age eighteen, alone and without knowing a word of English, he left Russia and went to the United States. Nehemiah ended up in Chicago, working mainly as a tailor. He spent much of his free time with other poor Jewish workers who were interested in socialism and Zionism. They belonged to a group called Workers of Zion.

Although Nehemiah was very impressed with America, and especially with American democracy, he decided that his place was with the Jewish community in Palestine, which Jews called the *Yishuv*. In 1917, as World War I raged, he joined a newly formed group called the Jewish Legion and left America for Palestine. The Legion's goal was to help Allied forces free Palestine from Turkish control. Among its founders was David Ben-Gurion, who later became Israel's first prime minister. Years later Ben-Gurion told Yitzhak, "I recruited your father for the Jewish Legion, and that's why you were born in Palestine."[2]

By the time Nehemiah's unit arrived in Palestine most of the fighting against the Turks was over. In any event, the Allied victory in World War I removed Palestine from Turkish control. It was turned over to Great Britain by the League of Nations under what was called a mandate. According to the League's mandate system,

Britain was to govern Palestine until its people were ready for independence. One of its tasks was to make possible the "establishment of a Jewish National Home" in Palestine, an idea drawn from the Balfour Declaration issued by the British government in November 1917.[3] Exactly what that national home would look like, or what its borders would be, the Balfour Declaration did not say.

In 1920, when the British received their mandate, it included the entire region that today contains Israel, the West Bank and the Gaza Strip, the Golan Heights, and the Kingdom of Jordan. However, in 1921, the British separated what today is Jordan from Palestine and installed an Arab prince from the Arabian Peninsula as its ruler. They thereby closed about three-quarters of the original Palestine mandate to Jewish immigration. Two years later, in return for territory in Iraq, the British ceded the Golan Heights to the French-controlled mandate of Syria.

Four years after Nehemiah Robichov was born into poverty near Kiev, Rosa Cohen was born into a prosperous family in the town of Mogilev, in the part of the old Russian Empire that today is Belarus. Her father, a rabbi, opposed Zionism. He believed that Jews should await the Messiah promised in the Bible to lead them back to their ancient homeland. However, Rosa's uncle Mordechai was a convinced Zionist. During the 1870s and 1880s there were violent mob attacks on Jews in Russia known as pogroms. Severe government discrimination added to the hardship. As a result, several million Jews fled Russia between 1880 and 1914. Most went to the United States. A small minority decided to go to Palestine. In 1897, Rosa's uncle Mordechai and his family joined the migration eastward and settled in Jerusalem.

Rosa Cohen was an independent child. She convinced her father to let her attend a Christian secondary school for girls, then defied his wishes by attending classes on Saturday, the Jewish Sabbath. Rosa worked as a private tutor to pay her school fees. For years Rosa was attracted to socialism rather than to Zionism. She hoped that a socialist revolution in Russia would bring a better world for all people, whatever their religion. At the same time, Rosa stuck by her fellow Jews. After a pogrom in the town where she was going to school, Rosa became a medical assistant. She was not afraid to go out at night to help victims of mob violence.

In 1917 came the revolution that Rosa had hoped for. It turned out to be a bitter disappointment, however. The Bolshevik party that eventually seized power established a one-party dictatorship. In 1919, Rosa decided to leave Russia. She intended to go to America or Scandinavia, but the first ship she could find was headed for Palestine. On board were young Zionist pioneers who intended to build a new settlement in the northern part of the country near Lake Kinneret (the Sea of Galilee). Their idealism convinced her to join them. So, as with Nehemiah Rabin, Zionism brought Rosa Cohen to Palestine.

If Zionism brought Nehemiah and Rosa separately to Palestine, anti-Jewish violence brought them together in Jerusalem. By 1920, Jewish immigration into Palestine was encountering strong Arab opposition. The Arabs opposed Jewish immigration, even though many Arab residents of Palestine themselves were immigrants who had come to take advantage of job opportunities caused by Jewish economic activity. In April 1920, Arab mobs attacked Jews in the part of Jerusalem known as the Old City. Shouting "We shall drink Jewish blood," the mobs attacked the neighborhood known as the Jewish Quarter.

Nehemiah Rabin and other members of the Jewish Legion rushed from the town of Jericho to Jerusalem to defend their people. At that time Rosa Cohen was visiting her uncle Mordechai in his home in the new and main section of Jerusalem outside the Old City walls. Upon learning about the trouble in the Old City, she immediately put on a nurse's uniform and went to the Jewish Quarter to treat the wounded. It was there, in the middle of the rioting, that Rosa Cohen and Nehemiah Rabin met. A year later they were married in Haifa. Rosa kept her maiden name after her marriage. On March 1, 1922, she gave birth to a son, Yitzhak, in Jerusalem.

The Rabins settled in Tel Aviv, where their second child, Rachel, was born in 1925. Nehemiah went to work for the newly founded Palestine Electric Corporation, one of the most important Jewish-owned companies in the country. Rosa worked as an accountant for a large construction firm. Working near her as a cashier was Golda Meir, who later would become Israel's prime minister. Years later when Meir told Rabin she had been a cashier at the construction firm, he answered, "So was my mother." Golda, as Israelis called their grandmotherly prime minister, corrected him. "No. I was the cashier; your mother was the accountant."[4]

Earning a living was only a small part of Nehemiah's, and especially Rosa's, working day. Both parents were deeply involved in public affairs, "a duty owed to the community."[5] Nehemiah was active in trade-union activities at the Electric Company. Union meetings were held at the Rabin home, as were meetings related to Rosa's many activities. She was a virtual dynamo, involved in political and social work all over Tel Aviv. Rosa's main concern was the welfare of Tel Aviv's Jewish workers, but she had so many activities and obligations that she had to pin notes to her dress in order to remember them all.

No activity was more important than defending the Jewish community. Both Rabins belonged to the Hagana, which was founded in 1920. Military duties often took Nehemiah away from home for weeks at a time. Guns were stored and hidden in the Rabin apartment. Once, when a gun accidentally went off, a bullet almost hit Rachel.

Rosa was always on call, even when strolling with her children. "We would never get to our destination on time," Rabin remembered. "We were always being held up because on the way she would meet someone who took the opportunity to ask her something or to talk things over with her." Rachel, the younger child, at least took advantage of the delays. As she later recalled, "I used to pull on her dress, and she would buy me ice cream to keep me quiet."[6]

All these activities and commitments took a toll on the Rabin home life. Because the parents were so busy, the children often had to be cared for by neighbors, a situation that Yitzhak later admitted he did not like but understood. The only time reserved just for the family was Friday evenings, when the Jewish sabbath begins with a special meal. Still, the Rabin home was a happy place. Although Yitzhak's parents were not religious, they took great pride in being Jewish. They also stressed their socialist values by rejecting luxury and expecting their children to do chores. Waste was not tolerated. The chil-

*Six-year-old Yitzhak with his mother Rosa and sister Rachel.
Both children knew their mother had a heart condition and
were always careful not to upset her. Rosa died when
Yitzhak was in high school.*

dren helped make the beds, wash dishes, and sweep floors. They were taught that one "did not work merely to satisfy material needs; work was valuable in itself."[7]

Yitzhak's first school reflected his early training at home. It was a new school founded by workers' organizations in Tel Aviv called the Bet Hinuch (House of Education). The school was set up because working people in Tel Aviv who thought like Rosa were not satisfied with just teaching children basic academic subjects. They wanted to prepare children to be pioneers with the skills necessary to build new settlements and work the land. Bet Hinuch stressed practical training and socialist values. Along with their academic studies, students cooked their own meals, washed dishes, tended a vegetable garden, and worked in the school carpentry shop. To promote socialist egalitarianism, students called their teachers by their first names.

Students attended school six days a week. Many remained in school until 4 P.M. because of their parents' work schedules. Conditions were far from ideal, especially during the first years when the school was housed in a ramshackle wooden building. None of that bothered Yitzhak or the other students:

> *It was hot in the summer and wet in the winter, but we loved it, we loved the atmosphere that pervaded it. We loved to study in the hut—that is to say, on those days when it was possible to study—for if the flooding rose beyond a certain level, the students had to adjourn to the dining room.[8]*

When the school's facilities finally improved, it was, as usual, due in large part to Rosa's efforts. She ˢᵒᵐ⁻ ⁱ her uncle Mordechai to lend the school a large sum of money so it could move to better quarters. But a new building did not correct the academic weaknesses of Bet Hinuch. Nor were those weaknesses addressed after Yitzhak completed his studies and moved on to a regional intermediate school called Givat Hashalosha (Hill of the Three), which his mother had helped found. When he applied to enter high school Yitzhak found he was poorly prepared in mathematics and several other academic subjects. After failing his entrance examinations, he had to study hard for several months until he passed on his second try.

Yitzhak was a handsome boy with reddish-brown wavy hair, like his father. His intense eyes and facial expressions seem to have come from his mother. Yitzhak was strong and a good athlete who enjoyed sports, but also was very shy. He rarely spoke, whether in school or when he was with other children or adults. As he wrote in his memoirs, "Then, as now, I did not show my feelings or share them with others."[9] One feeling he hid was his concern for his mother. Rosa had a heart condition, and Nehemiah went into debt in a futile search for a doctor or treatment that could cure her.

In 1937 the family's dread became a reality. In October of that year Yitzhak became a student at the Kadoorie Agricultural High School. It was located in northern Palestine, far from Tel Aviv. In November he received an urgent message from his father to rush to Tel Aviv's Hadassah hospital. Rosa was dying. "I did not want to cry in front of her but I just couldn't help myself, and all my grief flooded out," Yitzhak remembered. More than 1,000 people attended Rosa's funeral in Tel Aviv. The principal of the Kadoorie school spoke for many when he wrote to the grieving Yitzhak:

Your mother was one of the great women of Israel whose names are associated with the idealism of the nation....May you find comfort in studying for the profession you have chosen, for your own good and for the good of the public which your mother loved so much and to which she gave so much of her time in her short life.[10]

Many years later, when Yitzhak entered politics, he found many supporters who still remembered him as "Rosa Cohen's son."

Yitzhak returned to school "with the feeling that I had crossed over the threshold to manhood." He dedicated himself to his studies and became the best student in his class. He fully intended to serve his country as a farmer. But Yitzhak's studies and plans were about to be interrupted by more pressing matters. In 1929, Yitzhak had lived through Arab riots and attacks on Jews. In 1936 a far more serious outbreak of riots and attacks on Jews began. It was organized by the Arab leadership in Palestine. The main issue behind what was called the "Arab Revolt" once again was Jewish immigration, which had surged upward after the Nazi rise to power in Germany. The Arabs attacked Jewish settlements as well as Jews living in cities. Several attacks were launched on the Kadoorie school. The British authorities did little to stop the attacks. The Jewish Yishuv would have to protect itself. Yitzhak Rabin's military career was about to begin.

Yitzhak had been taught how to use a gun as a thirteen-year-old student in intermediate school. Now the training became more serious. He and the other boys were trained by a Hagana sergeant—and Kadoorie graduate—named Yigal Allon. More intensive training followed at a nearby kibbutz when the British temporarily closed Kadoorie during 1938. Rabin's duties included guard duty and setting ambushes. Allon, who like Rabin became a leading Israeli general and politician, was impressed with Yitzhak's abilities:

> *He had a sort of analytical approach to problems.*
> *He would never say he understood something*
> *before he really did understand all that it involved.*
> *Once he said that he understood, you knew that*
> *he did.*[11]

By the time Rabin and his fellow students returned to school in October 1939, World War II had broken out. Yitzhak found it difficult to concentrate on his studies, but did well enough to graduate at the top of his class in 1940.

By 1940 the Arab Revolt was over, but the Yishuv faced far greater problems. The start of World War II and the German victories that followed directly threatened millions of Jews in Europe. Already in 1938, Chaim Weizmann, the leader of the world Zionist movement, had warned that for European Jews the "world is divided into places where they cannot live and into which they cannot enter."[12] The situation became dramatically worse in May 1939 when the British announced their White Paper of that year. The White Paper was specifically designed to win over Arab public opinion, which was becoming increasingly pro-German. It ignored the desperate plight of millions of Jews by limiting Jewish immigration into Palestine to 75,000 over the next five years. After that, all Jewish immigration would be

In 1940 Yitzhak graduated from high school, intending to become a farmer. Events overtook him and turned him into a soldier. Within one year of graduation Yitzhak became one of the first members of the Palmach, a fighting force set up to protect the Jewish community of Palestine.

banned. The White Paper also forbade Jews to buy land in 95 percent of Palestine.

The Jews in Palestine were shocked and bitterly angry. Nonetheless, more than 32,000 Palestine Jews served in the British armed forces fighting the Nazis. (More than 130,000 actually volunteered.) As Chaim Weizmann put it, "Their war is our war." In terms of British immigration policy, however, the attitude was different. The Jews of Palestine simply could not accept the White Paper, which amounted to a death sentence for the Jews in Europe and the end of any hope for a Jewish national home. David Ben-Gurion, head of the Jewish Agency, the governing organization of the Jewish community in Palestine, summed up its attitude when he said, "We shall fight the war as if there were no White Paper, and the White Paper as if there were no war."[13]

One way of fighting was to set up a full-time military force to protect the Jewish community. This became essential by 1941 as German victories in North Africa meant that Germany might overrun Palestine. The new force, set up by the Hagana, was called the Palmach. The threat to Palestine was so grave that the British did not stop its formation and even trained some Palmach soldiers for commando and scouting missions. One of the first young people recruited into the Palmach was Yitzhak Rabin, who at the time was living on a kibbutz. Several weeks after he agreed to join, a Hagana officer came to see him. The officer was Moshe Dayan, who was destined to become one of Israel's legendary war heroes. Dayan was looking for men to undertake a dangerous mission. He had no time and did not waste it conducting a long interview:

Do you know how to fire a rifle?
Yes.

Have you ever thrown a hand grenade?
Yes.

Do you know how to operate a machine-gun?
No.

Can you drive?
No.

Can you ride a motorcycle?
No.

All right. You'll do.[14]

Only nineteen, Rabin had just been accepted for a sabotage mission into Lebanon. Lebanon and Syria were under control of the French puppet government that the
Germans had set up after defeating and occupying France.
The British planned to invade Lebanon and Syria to stop
the Germans from using them as springboards to seize
the Middle East and its invaluable oil resources. They
sent in Palmach units first to destroy telephone commu-
nications lines, ambush enemy patrols, sabotage roads,
and blow up installations. The young Jewish soldiers were
warned that if they were caught they probably would be
shot on the spot. Rabin's unit was ordered to cut key
telephone wires:

> *The route to our objective was 30 miles (48*
> *kilometers)—to be covered on foot, of course. As the*
> *youngest, I was given the job of climbing up the*

telephone poles. We had received our climbing irons only that day and hadn't had time to practice. Unable to use the irons, I took off my boots (which was the way I was used to climbing), shinnied up the pole, and cut the first wire, only to find out that the pole was held upright by the tension of the wires. The pole swayed, and I found myself on the ground. But for a lack of choice, up again I climbed, cut the wire, made my way down, and repeated the operation on the second pole. Mission completed, we...made our way back...by a shortcut.[15]

The successful Palmach operations in Lebanon boosted its prestige, but its future remained uncertain. By 1943, as the Nazi threat to Palestine faded, the British turned against the Palmach and once again began arresting its men if they carried weapons. Nor was the Yishuv leadership overly enthusiastic about the Palmach. Many leaders believed that it cost too much to maintain and should be disbanded.

The Palmach leadership believed that its force had to stay together and remain prepared. Rabin was among those who were convinced that as soon as the war ended the Jews "would have to fight for our lives in Palestine" and that only an independent Jewish military force could give them a chance to survive.[16]

The organization was held together by a scheme in which Palmach members lived in kibbutz settlements, working half of the month for their keep and training or taking on military tasks the other half. It often was a monotonous routine and, as Rabin recalled, only "deep faith and inner conviction held the Palmach together."[17]

Led by Yitzhak Sadeh, a veteran of the Soviet Union's Red Army, the Palmach stressed individual initiative, speed, and aggressiveness in battle. Building on Hagana tactics of "active defense" developed in the 1930s, Palmach troops were trained to move quickly on patrol and attack day or night, before the Arab gangs could strike. The Palmach even managed secretly to start a naval program and a tiny air force disguised as a flying club.

Rabin meanwhile advanced into a leadership position. He became a platoon leader in 1943. One of his assignments was helping illegal Jewish immigrants cross into Palestine from the north. He earned a reputation as a first rate leader whose men were tough and well trained in hit and run tactics. Rabin also was known and highly respected as a thorough, careful, and innovative military strategist. Early in 1945, as World War II drew to a close, the Palmach reorganized its small force into several battalions. Rabin was made second-in-command of the First Battalion. He also was put in charge of training section leaders for the Palmach.

Rabin's personal life also advanced. In 1944 he met a pretty, dark-haired, blue-eyed fifteen-year-old schoolgirl in Tel Aviv named Leah Schlossberg. She had been born in Germany and immigrated to Palestine with her parents in 1933. Their first few encounters amounted to what Yitzhak remembered as "a glance, a word, a stirring within, and then a further meeting."[18]

According to Leah, after several wordless "meetings" she asked some friends the name of the good-looking young man with the "chestnut hair and beautiful eyes." Then she approached the "terribly shy" youth who reminded her of the Bible's King David and asked, "Your

name is Yitzhak?" After his one-word answer—"Yes"—
she added, "And I'm Leah."[19]

Matters proceeded slowly from there, in part because Yitzhak rarely had time off from the Palmach. In
1945, Leah graduated from high school and herself joined
the Palmach. She served in the battalion of which Yitzhak
was the deputy commander, "one of the rare occasions
in our life together when *she* was under *my* command,"
Rabin noted wryly.[20]

By then World War II finally was over. By 1943,
however, the Jews of Palestine had already learned that
the Nazis were engaged in the mass murder of European Jews. Now their worst fears were confirmed as the
unimaginably horrible toll of the Holocaust became
widely known: the Nazis had murdered six million Jews
in their campaign of genocide. But the Jewish community of Palestine barely had time to mourn. It had to do
what it could to help the few survivors. And, as Rabin
had foreseen, it had to fight for its life.

CHAPTER THREE

"Our war is just beginning."

The defeat of Nazi Germany in May 1945 removed the common enemy that had prevented a direct confrontation between the British and the Yishuv. They immediately clashed over two questions, each of which was critical to whether the Jews would have a national home in Palestine. First, what level of Jewish immigration would the British permit while they still controlled Palestine? Second, would the Jewish community be allowed to establish an independent state when and if the British were to leave Palestine?

The question of Jewish immigration brought the relations between the Yishuv and the British to the breaking point. With the war over, and in light of the catastrophe that had befallen the Jews of Europe, the Jews in Palestine expected the British to lift their White Paper restrictions. By the summer of 1945, it was clear that the

British govenment intended no such thing. In Europe 250,000 desperate Jewish refugees, among them tens of thousands of orphaned children, were wandering from place to place or waiting in "displaced persons" (DP) camps in Europe with no place to go. Yet the British government, increasingly pro-Arab in its outlook, ignored the pleas of the Jewish community in Palestine. It also ignored the request of U.S. President Harry Truman in August 1945 and the recommendation of a joint American-British committee in March 1946 to immediately allow 100,000 refugees into Palestine.

The Yishuv therefore decided to take matters into its own hands. Rabin and his comrades in the Palmach found themselves carrying out some of the most dangerous actions associated with that decision.

Beginning in mid-1945, agents from the Yishuv moved thousands of Holocaust survivors from DP camps to the coast of France and Italy. After walking for hundreds of miles, they sailed in battered and unsafe old boats for Palestine. Between 1945 and 1948, sixty-three ships sailed from Europe with their cargo of refugees. Only five made it. The rest were intercepted by gunboats and warships of the British navy off the coast of Palestine, within sight of the Promised Land. Often the refugees on the boats fought the British boarding parties. As the British towed their boat into Haifa harbor, one group unfurled a defiant banner that read as follows:

> *We survived Hitler. Death is no stranger to us.*
> *Nothing can keep us from our Jewish homeland.*
> *The blood be on your head if you fire on this*
> *unarmed ship.[1]*

This Hagana ship was seized by British naval units while attempting to land on the Palestine coast. The refugees were deported to Cyprus.

Neither fists nor banners could stop the British, who deported and imprisoned thousands of refugees from Hitler's deadly concentration camps on the island of Cyprus, and even sent some back to Germany. It was to prevent deportation that the Palmach sent Rabin and his comrades to liberate refugees from the Atlit camp in October 1945. That raid made him a hero to Palestine's Jews. It also made him a wanted man to the British.

Jewish defiance of the British went beyond smuggling refugees through the blockade. By the fall of 1945 armed Jewish units were attacking British soldiers and bases. Some of the attacks were launched by the mainstream Jewish community using the Hagana and the Palmach. Two smaller and more extreme organizations also turned on the British. One was called the Irgun. It was led by Menachem Begin, a Polish-born Jew who reached Palestine during World War II. In 1977, Begin would become Israel's prime minister. Even more militant than the Irgun was a tiny organization called Lehi, which the British called the Stern Gang.

One major Hagana strike against the British took place in June 1946 after the British intercepted a ship carrying more than 1,700 men, women, and children. The Hagana attacked British police stations and other targets throughout the country. An attack that never took place nonetheless knocked Rabin out of action and put him in the hospital. He was supposed to lead an assault on an important British police station in the town of Jenin. However, during the planning process, while rushing on his motorcycle to a meeting with Yigal Allon, Rabin hit a truck and broke his leg. He spent three weeks in the hospital and then was "sent home, hobbling on crutches. All I could do was to follow Palmach operations from an armchair, cursing my fate."[2]

*Menachem Begin in one of his first public appearances
is shown here with his "adjutant," a man who
dressed exactly like him presumably to foil would-be
assassins. Begin was at this point the leader of the Irgun,
a militant underground organization that broke away
from the Hagana in the 1930s. He later became leader of
the Likud party which was the leading opposition to
the party in power, Labor, in which Rabin became a
prominent figure after returning to Israel in 1973.*

Rabin was not in his armchair for long. On June 18, the Palmach blew up most of the bridges linking Palestine with its neighbors. The infuriated British retaliated by arresting more than 3,000 Hagana members over a two-week period. The British raids began on Saturday (the Jewish sabbath), June 29, a date Jews in Palestine have since called "Black Sabbath." Among those arrested were Nehemiah and Yitzhak Rabin. While Rabin was in prison the cast on his leg was removed, and he began an intensive exercise program to restore his badly withered leg to health. Finally, in November the prisoners were released.

At this point Rabin had to make a decision about his future. In 1940 he had declined a chance to study water engineering at the University of California at Berkeley because he decided that his place during World War II was in Palestine. Once again Kadoorie's star graduate had a chance to go to Berkeley. A conversation with Allon, the Palmach's commander, ended that possibility. "The World War has ended, but our war is just beginning," Allon said.[3] Rabin agreed, and one week later he took command of the Palmach's Second Battalion. In October 1947, Allon appointed Rabin deputy commander of the Palmach.

Between mid-1946 and the fall of 1947 the situation in Palestine changed drastically. Britain, exhausted by World War II and unable to stem the Jewish resistance in Palestine that was taking a growing toll on British soldiers, decided to give up its mandate and leave the country. The decision on what to do with Palestine was turned over to the United Nations Special Committee on Palestine (UNSCOP). It recommended dividing the country into a Jewish state and an Arab state.

Jerusalem would become an international zone, not part of either state. On November 29, 1947, the UN General Assembly formally approved the recommendation. A few days later, Britain announced it would leave Palestine on May 15, 1948.

Arabs both inside and outside of Palestine bitterly opposed the UN decision and the idea of a Jewish state in any part of Palestine. "Any drawn line by the United Nations will be nothing but a line of blood and fire," one Arab representative to the UN announced.[4] The reaction among the Jews was quite different. They were overjoyed at the chance to finally build a national home free of British interference. At the same time, they knew that they would face bitter and violent Arab opposition, not just from inside Palestine but from several neighboring Arab countries.

The Jewish community was hardly ready to face such a threat. Its population of approximately 650,000 was about one-third of the total in Palestine. The Arabs controlled most of the country's high ground. They also controlled the territory between the main concentration of the Yishuv's population and Jerusalem, where over 90,000 Jews were almost isolated. In addition, the Arabs were much more heavily armed than the Jews. Behind them stood the armies and heavy weapons of at least five Arab countries poised to invade Palestine when the mandate ended. The Arabs also were favored by the British, who when they withdrew from strategically important points often turned them over to Arab soldiers.

Against this, in April 1947 the Hagana had an arsenal that totaled about 10,000 rifles, 1,900 submachine guns, and 444 light machine guns. As Rabin observed later, "It goes without saying that there was not a single cannon, heavy machine gun, or antitank or antiaircraft weapon, not to mention armor, air, or naval force."[5] The Palmach numbered barely 2,000 troops. Another 1,000 soldiers stood in reserve. The Hagana had over 30,000 other troops, but they were not nearly as well trained as the Palmach. The Irgun and Lehi also had small armies, but for much of the war they acted on their own rather than under Hagana command.

Nor were the Jews given time to prepare. In essence, the War of Independence, which officially dates from May 15, 1948, began in late 1947. By then, Jews in Arab countries throughout the Middle East were in danger. During 1947 and 1948 there were murderous pogroms in Syria, Egypt, Libya, Iraq, and several other countries. The Jews of Palestine came under attacks from Arab terrorists. In December, Arabs murdered thirty Jews in Haifa. The worst incident occurred in February 1948 in Jerusalem, where 54 people died when terrorists blew up several buildings in the center of the city. Much more important, Arab forces moved to cut off the Jews of Jerusalem from the main Jewish areas along the Mediterranean coast and the city of Tel Aviv. They also tried to isolate Jewish communities in the Negev desert in the south and the Galilee region in the north.

Under Ben-Gurion's leadership, the Yishuv tried to resupply Jerusalem by sending convoys of trucks along the main road from Tel Aviv to Jerusalem. Arab snipers hidden in the hills ambushed the convoys and killed many of the drivers. Unless the Jews in Jerusalem were resupplied, the city would fall to the Arabs. In March, Ben-Gurion ordered the Hagana to clear the road to Jerusalem. The campaign was called Operation Nachshon. By April 6, after taking heavy losses, Jewish soldiers held enough key points so a convoy was able to reach Jerusalem. The

Palmach then was given the job of completing Operation Nachshon. It created a new unit for the job, the Harel Brigade, with Rabin as its commander.

Over the next month the 1,500-man Harel Brigade was involved in desperate and bloody fighting along the Jerusalem road and in Jerusalem itself. After briefly keeping the road open, the brigade was moved to Jerusalem, where 2,500 Jews living in the Jewish Quarter of the Old City were cut off from the modern western part of the city beyond the walls, where most Jews lived. The Harel Brigade was fighting to hold open the Jerusalem road, defend the new city, and link up with the besieged Jewish Quarter in the Old City.

It turned out to be an impossible assignment. Rabin's forces could not take a police fortress along the Jerusalem road at Latrun, which the British earlier had turned over to the Arabs. They were, however, able to take control of the center of Jerusalem when the British evacuated the city on May 14. But the Harel Brigade could not rescue the Jewish Quarter. It was a difficult time for Rabin, who had disagreed with military decisions made by others that turned out to be disastrous. His men became angry about the high rate of casualties, which by early May reached 100 dead and 400 wounded and would later go even higher. Some of them blamed their commander, adding to Rabin's pain.

Elsewhere, the tide of battle favored Jewish forces, whose numbers grew as the Hagana expanded its ranks. During April they took Haifa with its port on the Mediterranean, the town of Acre a few miles to the north, and the city of Tiberias on Lake Kinerret. On May 9–10, in house-to-house fighting, troops led by Yigal Allon seized the key mountain town of Safed. On May 14, the town of Jaffa near Tel Aviv was taken. These victories dramatically strengthened the Jewish position in critical parts of Palestine. Meanwhile, some new weapons purchased from Czechoslovakia were arriving, as were Jewish volunteers with military experience from several foreign countries.

As the fighting raged, on May 14, 1948, at a meeting at the Tel Aviv Museum, David Ben-Gurion read an announcement proclaiming "the establishment of the Jewish state in Palestine–to be called Israel."[6] Ben-Gurion's words announcing the first independent Jewish state in almost 1,900 years were broadcast on radio to Israel and the world. In its first act, Israel's new government revoked the White Paper of 1939. Henceforth, any Jew could enter and live in the new state. The government's first meeting lasted barely half an hour, at which point Ben-Gurion announced simply, "The State of Israel has arisen. The meeting is ended." That same day word arrived that the United States had become the first country to officially recognize the new state.

In most of Israel joyful people celebrated in the streets. At a kibbutz a few miles outside Jerusalem, Rabin and his exhausted soldiers had no energy to celebrate. As Ben-Gurion's voice came over the radio one weary soldier asked, "Hey, guys, turn it off. I'm dying for some sleep. We can hear the fine words tomorrow." As for Rabin:

> I was mute, stifling my own mixture of emotions. None of us had ever dreamed that this was how we should greet the birth of our state, but we were filled with an even stronger sense of determination now that the state existed.[7]

Israeli state officials listen as Prime Minister David Ben-Gurion reads the "Declaration of Independence," and the nation of Israel is born. The joy Israel felt was quickly muted as the very next morning, at dawn, the new state's Arab neighbors declared war and attacked both the southern and northern borders.

The Israelis would need all their determination. The next day, May 15, the armies of five Arab countries—Egypt, Syria, Lebanon, Transjordan, and Iraq—stormed into Israel, determined to destroy the infant state in its cradle. Azzam Pasha, the head of the Arab League to which they all belonged, left no doubt about their intent:

> *This will be a war of extermination and a*
> *momentous massacre which will be spoken of like*
> *the Mongol massacres and the Crusades.*[8]

At the time, it looked as if Pasha's prediction would come true. The Jews still had no weapons to match the tanks, artillery, aircraft, ships, and other heavy weapons of the invading Arabs. A few months before the invasion, the commander of British forces in Palestine expressed the generally accepted assessment when he said that Arab armies "would have no trouble in taking over the whole country."[9]

At dawn on May 15, Egyptian planes bombed Tel Aviv while its army attacked Israel from the south. In the north the armies of Syria, Iraq, Transjordan, and Lebanon crossed Israel's borders. The existence of the Jewish state clearly was threatened.

In Jerusalem, the Palmach and Rabin struggled desperately against Transjordan's Arab Legion, led by British officers, to save the Jewish Quarter in the Old City. At one point Rabin's men broke through to the Old City and delivered supplies and ammunition to the starving residents. But they could not hold out against the overwhelming odds and had to retreat. On May 28, Rabin was at the Palmach's strong point on Mount Zion, just outside the city walls. From there he witnessed a "shattering scene":

> *A delegation was emerging from the Jewish Quarter bearing white flags. I was horrified to learn that it consisted of rabbis and other residents on their way to hear the legion's terms for their capitulation. That same night the Jewish Quarter surrendered to the Arab Legion.*[10]

With the fall of the Jewish Quarter, the Western Wall, the last remaining part of the Second Temple of the ancient Israelites and the holiest site in Judaism, fell under Arab control. No Jew, Israeli or otherwise, would be allowed to visit the site until 1967, when Israel's soldiers under Rabin's leadership retook the Old City.

Meanwhile, the Egyptian army reached within 25 miles (40 kilometers) of Tel Aviv, despite heroic resistance by several Jewish settlements along its route. The Syrians pushed into the Galilee region, and Jordanian and Iraqi troops each held several key towns in the north and center of the country. Among them was Lydda, the country's only international airport.

Late in May the UN Security Council called for a ccase-fire. Israel agreed, but the Arabs did not. They demanded that Israel first renounce its independence. The Israelis, despite their military difficulties, told the Security Council:

> *If the Arab states want peace with Israel, they can have it. If they want war—they can have it too.*

*But whether they want peace or war, they can
have it only with the State of Israel.*[11]

By early June, Israel's resistance had stiffened and its
military situation, while still serious, stabilized. Most of
the Jewish settlements under attack had beaten off the
enemy. Jewish forces in the Galilee were pushing the
Arabs back. The Jewish state held most of the area assigned to it by the UN partition. Generally, Hagana
forces were better trained then their foes and much more
motivated. They were well aware, as Golda Meir put it,
that they had nowhere else to go if they lost this war.
Meanwhile, immigrants from the Cyprus detention
camps and experienced Jewish soldiers from other countries were arriving and joining Hagana units. New and
more powerful weapons purchased abroad also began
to arrive, including invaluable fighter aircraft from
Czechoslovakia.

Both sides then agreed to a truce, which took effect
on June 11. They used the truce to reinforce their military positions. During the truce the Israelis managed to
pave a path near the Tel Aviv-Jerusalem road that allowed them to bypass the Latrun fortress. Rabin had
learned of the path in May from one of his officers, who
claimed he could make it from Jerusalem to the coast
via a path that bypassed Latrun. Rabin sent three soldiers with the officer to test the route. When he was convinced it could be used, he suggested paving the route
instead of continuing the bloody and thus far futile attacks on Latrun. Once the path was paved, the route to
Jerusalem was secured permanently.

On July 8, a day before the truce was scheduled to
end, the Egyptian army resumed fighting. The Israelis

successfully struck back on several fronts. In a span of ten days they punched through Egyptian lines in the Negev, took the town of Nazareth in the Galilee, captured important towns near Tel Aviv, and seized territory near Jerusalem. They also used their new aircraft to bomb both Cairo and Damascus, the capitals of Egypt and Syria. On July 18, a second UN-sponsored truce began.

During the second truce the Israelis continued to reorganize and strengthen their position. Israel now had an official new army: the Israel Defense Forces (IDF). It was organized into four commands: the south, the coastal, Jerusalem, and the north.

Rabin also underwent what he called a "personal reorganization." On August 23, taking advantage of the respite provided by the second truce, he and Leah were married in Tel Aviv. The shy warrior, who had been fighting brutal battles for months, found the ceremony and formality of getting married nerve-wracking. When the rabbi scheduled to perform the ceremony was thirty minutes late, Rabin snapped, "This is the last time that *I'm* getting married."[12] It was, of course, as the marriage was a happy and fruitful partnership that lasted for the rest of Yitzhak's life.

A third round of fighting broke out in October 1948. It took place along the southern front commanded by Yigal Allon. The man he chose as his deputy commander was Yitzhak Rabin. The Israelis were looking for an excuse to fight. The Egyptian army was still in Palestine dangerously close to Tel Aviv and also positioned so that the Negev was virtually cut off from the rest of the country. The Egyptians gave them that excuse when they violated the truce by firing on an Israeli supply convoy. In

Yitzhak and Leah were married in the summer of 1948 during the second truce in the War of Independence. The young couple's new home was a small room in the apartment of Leah's parents in Tel Aviv.

seven days of hard fighting the Israelis opened the road to the Negev and captured its main town of Beersheba. They also forced the Egyptians to withdraw from territory along the Mediterranean coast back to what today is the Gaza Strip. However, powerful Egyptian forces still remained inside Palestine.

In December, Allon and Rabin again attacked the Egyptians. Advancing Israeli troops crossed into Egyptian territory in the Sinai Peninsula. They were on the verge of destroying the Egyptian forces facing them. But Allon and Rabin did not get to finish the job. International pressure caused Prime Minister Ben-Gurion to stop the Israeli offensive. Allon and Rabin were furious. They warned Ben-Gurion that allowing the Egyptians to escape with their forces intact and hold the Gaza Strip would trigger another war. Ben-Gurion stuck to his decision, and in early January a cease-fire took hold. In 1956 and again in 1967 events proved his two young officers to be right.

On January 13, 1949, Israel began armistice negotiations with Egypt on the island of Rhodes in the Mediterranean. An American diplomat, Dr. Ralph Bunche, took charge of the difficult negotiations, which began with the Egyptians refusing to meet with the Israelis face-to-face. Even when Bunche finally got the Egyptians into the same room with the Israelis, the Egyptians at first refused to speak directly with the Israelis. Rabin was part of the Israeli delegation, serving as an advisor to the Israeli diplomats who did the actual negotiating. Before he left, Allon told his deputy: "See to it that no agreement is reached which is less than peace. And don't agree to anything that gives us less than Gaza."[13]

Rabin was part of the delegation that hammered out an armistice with Egypt, but he was not at all pleased with the final agreement, which he believed compromised Israeli security. Here Moshe Dayan stands by while a list of Egyptian prisoners to be repatriated is reviewed.

Rabin was unable to accomplish what Allon wanted. While at Rhodes he wrote to Allon that the Israeli diplomats were giving away too much. Rabin strongly disagreed with the Israeli decision to allow the Egyptians to remain in Gaza and the Jordanians in the mountain region south of Jerusalem. He disagreed with Israeli diplomats who thought that the agreements reached at Rhodes would lead to genuine peace talks. Rabin believed that they would lead to another war. Once again he was proven correct by subsequent events.

Rather less important but still annoying, while Rabin had "never worn a tie in my life" before leaving for Rhodes, ties were part of the expected attire at diplomatic negotiations. His efforts to learn how to tie one ended in failure. After someone tied it for him, Rabin learned how to loosen it enough to get it over his head without losing the knot. That way he could slip it back on when necessary. Somehow Rabin managed, although he remained "terrified at the prospect that the knot might come undone" during his entire stay at Rhodes.[14]

By the time the armistice agreement with Egypt was signed on February 24, Rabin was back in Israel. He participated in the very last part of the war against Jordanian forces, in which Israeli troops secured key parts of the Negev from the Dead Sea to the port of Eilat. Israel now held about 8,000 square miles (20,700 square kilometers) of Palestine, about 21 percent more than under the original UN partition plan. In March the new nation was admitted to the United Nations.

However, the Old City in Jerusalem, and with it the Western Wall, remained in Jordanian hands, while the Gaza Strip, dangerously close to Tel Aviv, was under Egyptian control. More than 6,000 Israelis, almost one percent of the total population, had died in the country's War of Independence. More than 30,000 had been wounded. Much of the country's best farmland, including many of its famous citrus groves, were damaged during the fighting. And the war had cost Israel more than $500 million dollars, which it did not have.

Yitzhak Rabin had played an important part in helping his country survive its stormy birth. He now had to decide what role he should play to help it grow and flourish.

CHAPTER FOUR

"We built a mighty army."

The victory in the War of Independence left the Israeli people and government no time to rest. Immense tasks of nation building lay before them. The most immediate and urgent problem was bringing hundreds of thousands of refugees into the country, and once they were there, finding them homes and integrating them into Israeli society. The task was gigantic. Between 1948 and 1951, 687,000 immigrants arrived in Israel. They came from many different places and circumstances, almost all involving great hardship and suffering. Many were Holocaust survivors from DP camps in Europe. Others came from European countries like Bulgaria and Romania, where large numbers of Jews had survived the Holocaust, and non Arab Muslim countries like Turkey and Iran.

In addition, Jews from Arab countries began their massive immigration to Israel. The Jews of Yemen and Iraq, the two oldest Jewish communities in the world outside of Israel, came in two remarkable airlifts. They left behind cruel persecution and all their property. They were soon followed by the majority of the Jewish communities of Egypt and the other Arab countries in North Africa, who had endured centuries of discrimination punctuated by periodic outbursts of violence. By 1953 the Jewish population in Israel had gone from its 1948 figure of 650,000 to almost 1.5 million.

The early days of independence were extremely difficult. Refugees with no education or property waited in tent camps while a frantic effort was made to build new housing, often entire settlements, help people find work, provide social services, and more. Economic conditions were hard for veteran Israelis as well.

Meanwhile, Israel remained surrounded by enemies determined to destroy it. None of Israel's Arab neighbors was willing to make peace. They sponsored terrorist raids across Israel's borders in which hundreds of civilians were murdered over the next several years. The Arab League vigorously enforced an economic boycott of Israel, while Egypt, in violation of international law, barred Israeli ships and cargoes from the Suez Canal. In another violation of international law, Egypt also blockaded the Straits of Tiran at the southern end of the Gulf of Aqaba (which the Israelis call the Gulf of Eilat). This prevented Israel from using its port at Eilat to trade with Asia and Africa. The prevailing Arab attitude toward Israel was summed up in 1954 by the Egyptian foreign minister:

> *The Arab people are not embarrassed to declare:*
> *We shall not be satisfied except by the obliteration*
> *of Israel from the map of the Middle East.*[1]

Like many Israelis at this difficult time, Yitzhak Rabin stood "at a crossroads in my personal life." Once again he postponed, permanently as it turned out, his plans to go to the United States to study water engineering. Rabin felt what he called "a debt of honor toward the men whose courage and bodies had blocked the Arab advance." That is why he and other military officers made a commitment to "dedicate our lives to ensuring the State of Israel would never again be unprepared to meet aggression." While some Israeli leaders built up the new government and others provided vital social services, all accomplishing remarkable feats, none performed a more vital task for the new nation than Rabin and his comrades. As he put it, simply, "We built a mighty army."[2]

As he helped to build Israel's army, Rabin found out that political and personal conflicts often got in the way. The most important political issue for Rabin was the status of former Palmach officers such as himself. In 1948, Prime Minister Ben-Gurion had ordered the Palmach disbanded and its units integrated into the newly formed military command, the Israel Defense Forces (IDF). Ben-Gurion did not entirely trust the "Palmachniks," as they were called, because of their intense loyalties to each other and because many of them were associated with a different political party than the prime minister's. In October 1949 he even banned all IDF officers from attending a Palmach farewell rally. To keep Rabin from attending, Ben-Gurion invited him to his home, supposedly to discuss military matters. After several hours of discussions the prime minister even took the unusual step of inviting Rabin to stay for dinner. Rabin declined. After Yitzhak returned home and changed clothes, he and Leah rushed to the rally.

Rabin received an official reprimand for attending the rally, a much lighter punishment than he originally expected. He also received a personal scolding from the IDF's commanding officer, Chief of Staff Ya'akov Dori. Actually, Rabin's real punishment seems to have been meted out over the long term, in the form of delayed promotions and slower career advancement.

Still, Rabin did advance. The IDF, which was thrown together ad hoc during the War of Independence, was in the process of turning itself into a modern professional army. One of its most important priorities was training new officers. Rabin played a leading role in that project, and in 1950 he was promoted to the rank of colonel. In 1951 the new chief of staff Yigael Yadin, who also was a world-famous archaeologist, made Rabin head of the IDF's operations division. This appointment brought Rabin into the IDF's general staff, the top circle of officers that ran the army.

Rabin now was responsible for a wide variety of critical tasks in preparing the Israeli army for war. One such task was organizing the reserves. Because Israel had such a small population, it could not have a large standing army. Nonetheless, everyone who was able to do so served. All young people—men and women—entered the military at the age of eighteen. Young women served for a shorter period and did not go into combat. In addition, men remained in the reserves for many years after finishing their tour of duty, spending several weeks to a month in training each year. That way, if a war broke out, Israel could mobilize its reserves and immediately increase the size of its army by many times to face the far greater Arab standing armies. Rabin had the job of organizing this system that was so critical to the functioning of Israel's citizen army and its ability to assure the country's survival.

A year before becoming head of the operations division, Rabin took on another important job—that of father—when his daughter Dalia was born in 1950. In 1955, Leah and Yitzhak had a son, Yuval. In 1952 the Rabins moved to a modest home in Zahala, a suburb of Tel Aviv where many other military officers also chose to live. With the exception of a two-year stint as a teacher of English, Leah remained at home with the children. This was very important to Yitzhak. He wanted his children to have the full-time mother he had missed because of Rosa Cohen's many outside activities. Leah explained her decision:

> *I felt, though he never said it, that it was important for Yitzhak to know that I was home with the children, and that enabled him to throw himself body and soul into whatever he was doing....I sensed that if anything compensated for his own childhood, and for the immense effort invested in what he did, it was the security of knowing that I was at home on a "full-time job."*[3]

During 1952–1953 the Rabins spent nine months in Britain, where Yitzhak studied at the British army's Royal Staff College in Camberley. Upon returning home he became the IDF's director of training. That position gave him his first chance to visit the United States to study American methods, which greatly impressed him. One American training method that Rabin adopted was to have all officers take either commando or paratroop training. However, when he followed his own regulations and took paratroop training, he had to keep his activities secret from his pregnant wife. With good reason he suspected that she would not approve of her husband jumping out of airplanes.

In 1954, Moshe Dayan, the new chief of staff, promoted Rabin to the rank of major-general. In 1956, Rabin moved from the general staff back into the field when he accepted the post as head of the northern command.

Rabin's new assignment made him responsible for dealing with the constant tension along the border with Syria. However, in 1956 the real action was in the south. Beginning in 1955, terrorist raids from the Egyptian-controlled Gaza Strip and Jordan increased dramatically. Many Israeli civilians were killed and wounded, and a great deal of property was destroyed. Retaliatory raids across the border by the Israeli army did not stop the terrorism, and Israeli complaints to the UN brought no relief.

Meanwhile, Egypt used its artillery at the Straits of Tiran to block all shipping to and from Eilat. Egypt's aggressive and vigorous new military dictator, Gamal Abdel Nasser, began buying new weapons from the Soviet bloc and openly threatening Israel with destruction. "There will be no peace on Israel's border," he warned in August 1955, "because we demand vengeance, and vengeance is Israel's death."[4]

As a result, Israel decided that it had no choice but to attack Egypt, wipe out the terrorist bases in Gaza and the Sinai, and end the illegal blockade at the Straits of Tiran that was choking its economy. The attack began on October 29, 1956. Israel acted in cooperation with Britain and France, who had their own disputes with Egypt over the Suez Canal. The Israeli army swept into the Sinai Desert, overwhelmed the Egyptian army, and occupied the Egyptian positions at the Straits of Tiran. However, heavy pressure from both the United States and the Soviet Union forced an Israeli withdrawal from the Sinai in 1957. But the Israelis did not return home empty-handed. A United Nations peace-keeping force was placed in the Sinai to keep the straits open and prevent terrorist attacks across the border. It fulfilled its mission for the next decade.

Rabin had no direct involvement with the Sinai campaign. After it was over he still had to deal with the Syrians, whose army looked down on northern Israel from a rocky ridge called the Golan Heights. The Syrians turned the Golan into a fortress, bristling with bunkers and artillery. While UN observers did nothing to stop them, the Syrians on the Golan shelled Israeli settlements at will, raining terror and destruction on the civilians below. In Rabin's account:

> *Exposed to Syrian artillery, our citizens were forced to build shelters, adapt buildings to wartime conditions, and disperse their homes, kindergartens, schools, and public buildings to diminish their vulnerability. Matters reached the point where we were forced to use armored tractors—often manned by soldiers—to cultivate the fields. We also had to deal with safeguarding our fishing rights…while the Syrian army harassed our fishing boats.[5]*

There also were several pitched battles between Israeli and Syrian army units.

By 1959, Rabin had been passed over for promotion several times and was questioning whether he should continue his army career. Then a major blunder during a national drill in calling up reserves—the public was not told it was only a drill and thought that Israel was on the brink of war—led to a shake-up of the IDF's top command. Rabin suddenly found himself as the IDF's second-ranking officer. He also received a promise from Ben-Gurion that he would be Israel's next chief of staff.

At about the same time, Rabin had what he considered his first clash with Shimon Peres, who was then deputy minister of defense. It was the beginning of a rivalry that often became personal and bitter and that would last for more than thirty years. In fact, the two men even disagreed about when they had their falling out: Rabin dated their conflict from the early 1960s, while Peres said the tension began in the 1970s. Ironically, it was not until the two strong-willed and ambitious Israelis combined to try to make peace between their country and the Arabs that they finally were able to make peace between themselves.

Late in 1963, David Ben-Gurion retired from public life. His successor was Levi Eshkol, who had served as Israel's finance minister under Ben-Gurion. One of Eshkol's first decisions was not to extend the term of the IDF chief of staff he inherited from Ben-Gurion. In his place he appointed forty-one-year-old Yitzhak Rabin. His term of office began on January 1, 1964. By the time it ended, he had emerged as one of his country's greatest heroes.

As chief of staff, Rabin focused on several issues. He had to deal with the Syrians, who "kept the border in turmoil by employing artillery and armor" against the Israelis.[6] Along with protecting Israeli civilians from attack, Rabin had to safeguard against sabotage Israel's massive project to pipe water from Lake Kinneret to the dry south. In January 1965 the Israelis thwarted an attempt to blow up one of the project's aqueducts.

Rabin also had to protect water flowing into Israel. In 1965, with Arab League backing, Syria began a project to divert tributaries of the Jordan River, a project that if completed would have left Israel without vital water resources. Rabin's job was to find a way to destroy the Syrian earthmoving equipment without the risk of setting off a war. He summoned Major-General Israel Tal and asked him if tanks shooting from the Israeli side of the border could hit the Syrian targets about a mile away. Tal, as Rabin recalled, "flung himself into the task" and concluded that it could be done.[7] When Rabin asked for a "guarantee" of success, Tal, a man of immense confidence as well as talent, replied: "The guarantee is that I will aim and fire the tank *personally*."[8] Tal was good to his word, and the Syrians had to abandon the diversion project.

Most immediately threatening, Syria and Egypt were buying huge quantities of modern Soviet arms, including tanks. Rabin knew the IDF would need the most modern weapons available so Israel's armed forces would have a "qualitative edge" against their far more numerous enemies. The Israelis already had purchased modern jets from France, but Rabin insisted that only arms from the United States could match what the Arabs were getting from the Soviets. Prime Minister Eshkol agreed. During Rabin's tenure as chief of staff Israel bought a variety of modern American weapons. The weapons included advanced tanks and, for the IDF air force, Skyhawk combat planes, which could carry four times the bomb load of French planes. The Israelis were very pleased with the purchase, although unhappy that the United States also decided to sell tanks to Jordan.

In light of the new weapons, Rabin restructured the IDF. He divided it into two sections, offensive and defensive, equipping each section according to its tasks. To increase speed and mobility, the IDF's offensive forces stressed armored and motorized units and paratroops, along with regular infantry. The air force was to focus first on gaining air superiority if war broke out, and then to support ground forces. Rabin's restructuring of the military and introduction of new weapons turned out to be the right moves at the right time.

The year 1966, however, brought Israel plenty of trouble. The Syrians increased the pace of border attacks involving sabotage and shootings. An IDF reprisal raid against a terrorist base inside Jordan turned into a major clash with Jordanian troops. One incident with Syria that did not involve shooting brought Rabin and two of his top commanders—chief of operations Ezer Weizman and head of the northern command David Elazar—almost face to face with the Syrians. They were at Lake Kinneret when an Israeli fishing boat ran aground near the eastern shore of the lake. Although the lake itself was in Israeli territory, Syrian-controlled territory began only a few yards from shore.

In typical Israeli fashion—officers are expected to lead their troops into battle, not just order them in—the three commanders mounted their own rescue effort. Their "disguise" in an operation that took them to within 50 yards (46 meters) of Syrian soldiers, who actually photographed them, was to shed their uniforms for bathing trunks. Why the Syrians did not open fire on the stranded Israelis and their would-be rescuers remains a mystery. In any event, the three Israeli generals were not successful. A navy ship had to be called to tow the fishing boat to safety.

By the 1960s it was customary for the IDF chief of staff to serve a three-year term, so 1966 could have been Rabin's last year at his post. However, Prime Minister Eshkol asked Rabin to serve another year. When Rabin agreed, his decision put squarely on his shoulders the burden of defending Israel against the greatest threat to its survival since the War of Independence.

The crisis began in mid-May, just over a month after an air battle in which Israeli planes shot down six Syrian Soviet-built MIG fighter aircraft. As the Syrians turned to Egypt for help, the Soviet Union passed on false information to the Arabs that Israel was about to attack Syria. Egypt's president, Gamal Abdel Nasser, determined to prove he could deal with Israel, responded with a series of steps. On May 14 he began sending tens of thousands of troops and hundreds of tanks into the Sinai Peninsula, heading for the Israeli border. He then demanded that the UN peace-keeping force along the Egyptian-Israeli border withdraw. As Rabin succinctly put it, "The chariots of war were beginning to roll."[9]

Much to everybody's shock, including Nasser's, UN Secretary-General U Thant agreed. UN troops abandoned their posts along the border, in the Gaza Strip, and at Sharm el-Sheikh, a fortified position overlooking the Straits of Tiran from which Egyptian guns had enforced the blockade of Eilat prior to 1956. The UN troops left on May 19th. Three days later, Nasser announced a renewal of the blockade, a step that Israel considered an act of war.

Thus began a nerve-wracking period in Israel known as the "Hamtana," or waiting period. Israel turned to the world for help: to the United States, which in 1957, in return for Israel's withdrawal from Sinai, had promised to take responsibility for keeping the Tiran Straits open; to France, its most important supplier of arms up to that point; and to the UN, which for ten years had helped prevent a new war in the region. It received no help from any of them: no help in opening the straits from the United States, no promised arms from France, and no decisive action from the UN.

The Israelis were in a bind. They had been taken by surprise, they had no outside help, and events were moving incredibly fast. They could not afford to let Egypt and Syria, possibly aided by Jordan, strike first. Tiny in area, only 9 miles (14 kilometers) wide at its narrowest point, and facing a war on three fronts, Israel would then become a battleground. Its civilians would suffer enormous casualties. Visions of the Holocaust haunted Israel. So did statements like the one that Nasser made in 1965, when he promised the Arab world: "We shall not enter Palestine with its soil covered in sand. We shall enter it with its soil saturated in blood."[10]

But if Israel struck first, how would the world react? The Soviet Union supported the Arabs and was hostile to Israel. The United States was friendly to Israel, but also was courting the oil-rich Arabs, and had taken a leading role in forcing Israel to leave the Sinai Peninsula in 1957. France already was turning against the Israelis.

Meanwhile, Rabin experienced his own personal crisis. He had been under tremendous pressure for over a week, especially since Prime Minister Levi Eshkol and other politicians running the country seemed indecisive.

They all seemed to be turning to him to make the key decisions. As he put it later: "I was put in a position where the Government was saying: 'What do you want us to do? You have to tell us.'"[11]

On May 23 the pressure became too great. Israel was mobilizing for war. Rabin returned home "in a state of physical and mental exhaustion."[12] He was plagued by doubt. Had he prepared the IDF sufficiently for this crisis? How many thousands of young men would be killed or wounded, even if Israel prevailed in the coming struggle? That night Rabin seems to have suffered a nervous collapse. When Ezer Weizman visited him at home Rabin asked, "Am I to blame? Should I relinquish my post?"[13] Weizman tried to calm his chief of staff, first warning him, "If you resign now, you'll be finished for the rest of your life." He then added, "You'll be the victorious chief of staff. You'll reach the Suez Canal and the Jordan."[14]

A doctor was called to the scene. He gave Rabin sleeping medication, and the chief of staff slept until 3 P.M. the next morning. Rabin awoke refreshed and by the next day had returned to full activity. He had a great deal to do.

While the military prepared, Israel's diplomats desperately struggled to find backing abroad that would lead to a peaceful solution to the crisis. Prime Minister Eshkol stated his policy: "The IDF will not attack before the political options are exhausted."[15] Meanwhile, Egyptian troops continued to pour into Sinai, Iraqi troops arrived in Syria, and the noose around Israel was tightening. Rabin and his generals warned that time was running out. The IDF's intelligence chief, Aharon Yariv, warned: "Every passing day lessens the chances of Israel attaining air superiority," which was vital for achieving victory.[16] At one meeting, where action was delayed yet again, one general angrily shouted at the politicians, "What are we waiting for?"[17]

On May 30, Jordan signed a military pact with Egypt, meaning that Israel faced a war on three fronts. Arab leaders from Cairo to Baghdad echoed Nasser, who announced the Arab goal was to "totally exterminate the State of Israel for all time."[18] In Cairo huge crowds shouted: "Nasser, Nasser, Nasser, we are behind you. We will slaughter them. We will destroy them. Slaughter, slaughter, slaughter."[19]

By May 31, Egypt had 100,000 men, 1,000 tanks, and 500 heavy guns along Israel's border. As June dawned, Arab forces massed along Israel's borders outnumbered its own army by three to one. With the drumbeat of Arab threats and hatred in their ears, amplified by the deafening silence of the international community, Israelis prepared to fight for their country's survival. On May 31, the leading opposition political parties joined the government, thereby creating a regime of national unity. It included Menachem Begin and, significantly, Moshe Dayan, the hero of the 1956 Sinai victory, who became minister of defense on June 1. That same day it became incontestably clear that all political options were exhausted. The word came from Washington that the United States, Israel's last hope, would not take decisive action. Israel stood alone. On June 4, the Israeli government made the final decision to strike.

The war known as the Six-Day War began at 7:45 A.M. on June 5, 1967. Wave after wave of Israeli planes attacked Egyptian air bases, destroying most of the air force of Israel's most powerful enemy on the ground.

This photo of Israeli infantrymen was taken on May 31, 1967, as they marched to defend their country. They were outnumbered three to one by Arab forces massed along Israel's borders.

Of Israel's 200 combat aircraft, only twelve remained behind to protect Israeli air space. In the words of air force chief Motti Hod, "We used all we had."[20] And they used it again and again. Israeli planes operated on a precise time table: 22.5 minutes to reach their Egyptian targets, 8 minutes to attack, 20 minutes to return to base, 7.5 minutes to rearm and refuel, and then back to phase one. That left exactly two minutes as a safety margin to correct for the unexpected.

The bold gamble paid off. Within three hours the attack on Egypt was completed. Israeli planes then bombed airfields in Jordan and Syria with similar success. As the air battle unfolded, Rabin studied Motti Hod, the man who had prepared the air force for this day and who had dared to take the risks and predict success:

> *Was he excited? Did his face show any...hint of "I told you so?" I was so pleased with him, and for him....But his features were rocklike in their impassivity; not a muscle moved. He gulped down incredible amounts of water and held his tongue.*[21]

Despite the brilliant air victory that decided the course of the war, Israel did not escape unscathed. On June 5 Syrian, Jordanian, and Iraqi planes bombed the country. Tel Aviv and Rabin's own neighborhood of Zahala were among the places shelled by artillery from the Jordanian-held town of Kalkilia, only 11 miles (18 kilometers) away. As he fled with his mother for shelter, young Yuval Rabin told her, "I want to be where my father is."[22] In the north, Syria's Soviet-built MIG fighters strafed Haifa. In the east, Jordanian infantry and tanks advanced in and around Jerusalem while its artillery pounded the city.

Meanwhile, Israeli troops, supported by the air force that attacked the Egyptian army from the air, swept into the Sinai. Their overwhelming victory in the desert sometimes has obscured the fact that the Israelis in the Sinai faced bitter fighting and suffered many casualties. General Ariel Sharon, by that time a hardened veteran of two wars, described a key battle and Israeli victory that took place on the fourth day of the war:

> *This was the Valley of Death. I came out of it an old man. Hundreds were killed. There were burning tanks everywhere. One had the feeling that man was nothing. A sandstorm had been churned up by our tanks. The noise was tremendous. Besides the din of tanks and guns, there was the roar of our aircraft…dropping supplies of water and ammunition by parachute, and of helicopters evacuating the wounded. The shooting and fighting continued, and vehicles loaded with fuel and ammunition were exploding all along the line.[23]*

On that day, Israeli forces reached the Suez Canal. Ironically, Sharm el-Sheikh, where the Egyptian blockade on Israeli shipping did so much to cause the war, fell without a single shot being fired. The Egyptians retreated from that post hours before the Israelis arrived there on June 7. Rabin was both surprised and delighted to hear from the Israeli commander on the spot: "There's no one to fight."[24]

Fighting in Jordanian-controlled territory known as the West Bank also was hard. As in Sinai, however, Israel's control of the air enabled its army to rout the

Jordanians. Much of the toughest fighting took place in the battle for Jerusalem's Old City. The Israelis first attacked Jordanian fortifications in East Jerusalem outside the Old City on June 6. Israeli paratroopers fought Jordanian soldiers hand-to-hand until those positions fell. On June 7 at 8:30 A.M. the Israelis broke into the Old City. Paratroopers under the command of Colonel Mordechai ("Motta") Gur, a future chief of staff, headed for the Temple Mount and its Western Wall. The Jordanians used one of the mosques on top of the Temple Mount as a sniping post, and had turned the Mount itself into an ammunition dump. About 10 A.M. Gur radioed back to his commanders: "The Temple Mount is in our hands."

Early that afternoon Rabin and Moshe Dayan arrived from Tel Aviv at the Lion's Gate, one of the entrances to the Old City. They marched together with General Uzi Narkiss, the overall commander of the Jerusalem operation, to the Western Wall. Rabin recalled the extraordinary experience:

> As we made our way though the streets I remembered from childhood, pungent memories played on my emotions. The sheer excitement increased as we came closer to the Western Wall itself. It is still easy for me to conjure up the feelings that assaulted me, but it's very difficult to put them into words. The Wall was and is our national memento of the glories of Jewish independence in ancient times. Its stones have a power to speak to the hearts of Jews the world over, as if the historical memory of the Jewish people dwelled in the cracks between those ancient ashlars. For years I secretly harbored the dream that I might play a part not only in gaining Israel's independence but

From left, General Uzi Narkiss, Defense Minister Moshe Dayan, and Chief of Staff Rabin march proudly through the Lion's Gate into the Old City. As Rabin recalled, "I knew that never again in my life would I experience quite the same peak of elation."

*in restoring the Western Wall to the Jewish
people....Now that dream had come true, and I
suddenly wondered why I, of all men, should be
so privileged.*

*When we reached the Western Wall I was
breathless. It seemed as though all the tears of
centuries were striving to break out of the men
crowded in that narrow alley, while all the
hopes of generations proclaimed, "This is no
time for weeping! It is a time for redemption,
for hope." Following an ancient custom, Dayan
scrawled a wish on a piece of paper and pushed
it between two of the stones. I felt truly shaken
and stood there murmuring a prayer for peace.
Motta Gur's paratroopers were struggling to
reach the Wall and touch it. We stood among
a tangle of rugged, battle-weary men who were
unable to believe their eyes or restrain their
emotions. Their eyes were moist with tears,
their speech incoherent. The overwhelming
desire was to cling to the Wall, to hold on to
that great moment as long as possible.*[25]

Yet there remained more fighting, especially in the north.
The Golan Heights remained in Syrian hands, and the
thousands of people from the Galilee region to the Jordan River valley who had lived for years under their
murderous guns were demanding that their tormenters
be dislodged. A delegation of Galilee residents came to
Tel Aviv and told their national leaders:

*The Syrians are riding on our backs. If the
State of Israel is incapable of defending us,
we're entitled to know. We should be told*

outright we are not part of this state, not entitled to the protection of the IDF. We should be told to leave our homes and flee from this nightmare.[26]

The government hesitated, primarily because some ministers were concerned that if Israel attacked Syria the Soviet Union would intervene in the war. However, most Israelis agreed that the situation in the north was intolerable. Therefore, having defeated the Egyptians and Jordanians, Israel's leaders ultimately decided to risk attacking the Syrians. On June 9, Israeli soldiers attacked the entrenched Syrians on the Golan Heights. The troops were skillfully led by General David ("Dado") Elazar. But the Syrians, with the advantage of the fortified high ground, fought back and the Israelis suffered many casualties, including more than 100 dead. By June 10 the Golan Heights was in Israeli hands. A cease-fire was in place. The Six-Day War was over.

The war yielded Israel enormous gains. The Israelis held all of Jerusalem, and annexed the Old City and the rest of East Jerusalem (as the part of the city formerly held by Jordan was called) on June 28. They also held the Golan Heights, the Gaza Strip, and the Sinai Peninsula. Altogether, the 1967 cease-fire lines put Israel in control of some 26,000 square miles (67,340 square kilometers), more than three times the territory it controlled before the war. In addition, the victory restored the country's confidence, which had been severely shaken in the weeks before the war.

Israel paid dearly for these gains. The IDF suffered at least 777 dead and 2,586 wounded, enormous figures for such a small country. Civilian casualties brought the total of dead and wounded to more than 800 to 3,000,

Rabin and Dayan at the taking of the Golan Heights on the last day of the Six-Day War. This final territorial gain was very costly to Israel as the Syrians defending the Heights were deeply entrenched, but it provided vital security for Israel's northern settlements.

respectively. And, as Rabin pointed out, Israeli gains brought with them enormous problems. Israel now ruled over one million hostile Arabs living in the West Bank and the Gaza Strip. Furthermore, Rabin understood that Israel would not be left in peace to deal with its territorial gains.

Rabin made all this clear when he accepted an honorary doctorate from the Hebrew University in Jerusalem on June 28. He felt awkward, as the IDF does not award decorations to its senior officers. However, Rabin decided to accept the honor so he could talk about the unique nature of Israel's citizen army:

> *The elation of victory has seized the whole nation.*
> *Yet among the soldiers themselves a curious*
> *phenomenon is to be observed. They cannot rejoice*
> *wholeheartedly. Their triumph is marred by grief*
> *and shock, and there are some who cannot rejoice*
> *at all. The men in the front lines saw with their*
> *own eyes not only the glory of victory, but also its*
> *cost: their comrades fallen beside them, soaked in*
> *blood. And I know that the terrible price the*
> *enemy paid has also deeply moved many of our*
> *men. Is it because neither their teaching nor their*
> *experience has ever accustomed the Jewish people*
> *to exult in conquest and victory, that they receive*
> *them with such mixed feelings?* [27]

Whatever his own ambivalent feelings, Rabin emerged from the Six-Day War as a hero to his country. At the same time, he knew that his term as chief of staff and therefore his military career was almost over. His mind turned to building a new civilian career that would permit him to continue serving his country.

C H A P T E R   F I V E

"You're no diplomat!"

Even before the Six-Day War, Rabin was thinking about what to do when his term as IDF chief
of staff, and his military career, came to an end.
Rabin had a well-deserved reputation of being direct and
blunt. So when he suggested to Prime Minister Eshkol
that he be appointed Israel's next ambassador to the
United States, the response was a little less than encour-
aging. "Hold on to me, Yitzhak, or I'll fall out of my
chair," Eshkol blurted out, adding, "You're no diplomat!"[1] Nor was Rabin's command of English particularly good, especially compared with Israel's two
previous ambassadors to the United States, both of whom
were native English speakers born in South Africa.
Unfazed, Rabin renewed his efforts to be appointed to
the post after the war. Despite strong competition for the
desirable position, he was appointed and began preparing to take his post as of March 1968.

Before Rabin arrived in America, the diplomatic and political situation that he would face as a result of the Six-Day War was beginning to take shape. Within Israel, the overwhelming conviction was that the country could never return to the 1967 borders that had left it so insecure. Only two days after the war ended, Prime Minister Eshkol told Israel's parliament:

> *Let this be said—there should be no illusion*
> *that Israel is prepared to return to the conditions*
> *that existed a week ago—We have fought alone*
> *for our existence and our security, and we are*
> *therefore justified in deciding for ourselves what*
> *are the genuine and indispensable interests of*
> *our state, and how to guarantee its future.*[2]

At the same time, Israel hoped to be able to negotiate with its Arab neighbors to return much of the captured territory in exchange for peace. The Israelis insisted that this required direct negotiations between themselves and the Arabs and genuine peace treaties, not the indirect negotiations as in 1949 at Rhodes and the continued state of war and cease-fire that existed between 1949 and 1967.

One issue alone was not negotiable: Jerusalem would be united and under its rule. Moshe Dayan spoke for most of his countrymen when, entering the Old City flanked by Rabin and Uzi Narkiss, he announced, "We have returned to all that is holy in our land. We have returned never to be parted from it again."[3] What the Israelis found upon that return after being barred for nineteen years genuinely shocked them. The Jordanians had destroyed every Jewish house of worship in the Old City. They had even uprooted tombstones from Jewish graves in the ancient Mount of Olives cemetery and used them to pave army latrines. The Israelis pledged to allow Muslims and Christians to control their own holy sites. But the city itself would be united as the capital of Israel.

Given their overwhelming victory, the Israelis expected the Arabs finally would negotiate with them. As the saying went, they waited for a "phone call" from their neighbors. Instead of a phone call they received a rude awakening in August in the form of the infamous "three noes" announced at an Arab conference in Khartoum, Sudan: "No peace with Israel, no recognition of Israel, no negotiations with Israel."[4]

A more positive statement came from the United Nations Security Council on November 22. Its Resolution 242 called for Israel's withdrawal from "territories"— significantly, at the insistence of the United States, not *the* territories or *all* the territories—in return for a negotiated peace in which all nations in the region could live within secure and recognized boundaries. Israel, Egypt, and Jordan all accepted Resolution 242; Syria rejected it.

As Rabin was preparing for his new post in America, an important new player was emerging in the Arab-Israeli conflict: the Palestine Liberation Organization. The PLO was founded in 1964 on the initiative of the Arab League, when the West Bank, Gaza, and East Jerusalem all were under Arab rule. In its founding document, the Palestinian National Covenant, it called the establishment of Israel "null and void." In other words, the PLO denied Israel's right to exist, regardless of its borders. The PLO actually was an umbrella organization for a variety of feuding Palestinian groups united mainly by their determination to destroy Israel. After 1967 the most powerful group, known as Fatah, dominated the PLO, although it could not control the other groups that belonged to the organization. Fatah's leader, Yasir Arafat, an engineer who claimed he was born in Jerusalem but probably was born in Cairo, became the PLO chairman.

Over the next few years, Arafat's Fatah and other PLO groups committed hundreds of terrorist acts against Israeli civilians both inside and outside its borders, leaving many dead and wounded. Among the attacks that occurred while Rabin was in Washington was the mid-air bombing of a Swissair plane bound for Tel Aviv, killing all 47 people aboard. There also were several attacks on planes and passengers of Israel's El Al airline. On the ground, a May 1970 ambush of an Israeli school bus near the Lebanese border left twelve children and teachers dead. Perhaps the most publicized attack occurred during the 1972 Munich Olympic Games, when a PLO group closely tied to Fatah murdered eleven Israeli athletes.

Despite his inexperience and inadequate English, Rabin had an imposing agenda as he prepared to take his new post. A primary goal was to make sure that Israel could buy the arms it needed from the United States to balance arms the Arab states received from the Soviet Union. He had to secure American aid to cover at least some of these expensive purchases. Rabin also had to keep the United States sympathetic to Israel's approach for making peace. In particular, Israel insisted on direct negotiations with the Arabs, not a "solution" imposed on it by the American and Soviet superpowers, as the Arabs wanted. Israel also wanted the United States to support the idea that peace treaties should be negotiated *before* Israel withdrew from territories it held. This ran up against Arab and Soviet demands for the reverse: that Israel agree to a complete withdrawal prior to the start of peace negotiations. Israel also wanted the United States to prevent direct Soviet intervention on the Arab side if fighting broke out again in the turbulent Middle East.

Rabin's first difficulty actually emerged before he arrived in Washington. He and Leah agreed that their daughter Dalia would remain in Israel to complete her final year of high school. Then, like other Israeli eighteen-year-olds, she would enter the army. Although Dalia would be staying with Leah's sister and therefore was in "good hands," the parting was tearful for both mother and daughter. Yitzhak recalled:

> *I tried to remain stoic but I doubt I*
> *succeeded in hiding the ache that every*
> *father must feel when he sees his "little*
> *girl" going off into the world on her own.*[5]

Nor was it easy for him to accept, even as a former chief of staff, that he would be almost half a world away when his daughter was in the army.

When Rabin arrived in the United States in February 1968, he found a country in turmoil. The year 1968 marked the peak of the Vietnam War, which was increasingly unpopular with a large segment of the American population. Angry and sometimes violent demonstrations against the war were commonplace. Just after his arrival Rabin watched President Lyndon Johnson announce on television that he would not be a candidate for president in the upcoming November elections. Then came the assassination of Martin Luther King, Jr., on April 4. Rabin was stunned as he watched racial unrest turn into riots

Rabin, Israel's new Ambassador to the United States, presenting his credentials to President Johnson. Less than one month after this first meeting Martin Luther King, Jr. was assassinated. The riots and demonstrations growing out of anti-Vietnam war sentiments and the King assassination left Rabin deeply worried about the future of the country he called "this great democracy-the leader of the free world."[6]

and looting in several American cities, including Washington, D.C. To a "new and inexperienced ambassador, the situation looked depressingly grave."

On June 4, when Rabin was in New York, he was invited to meet with Robert F. Kennedy, who was campaigning for the Democratic party's presidential nomination. Tight scheduling prevented the meeting, which tragically never took place. The next day, the first anniversary of the outbreak of the Six-Day War, Kennedy was assassinated by a young Palestinian who was bitter about the senator's strong support for Israel.

As soon as he was settled, Rabin tried to convince the American government to sell Israel the ultramodern weapons it needed for defense. This was not an easy task. From the late 1940s until the late 1950s the Truman and Eisenhower administrations had refused to sell Israel any arms. Finally, in the late 1950s the Eisenhower administration sold Israel a few weapons. In the 1960s the Kennedy and then the Johnson administrations opened the arms spigot a bit more, but continued to refuse Israel's request for top-of-the-line fighter planes. Israel especially needed fifty American supersonic Phantom jets, the world's best and most powerful warplane. After long and complicated negotiations, a deal was reached in the fall of 1968. However, final approval from President Johnson did not come until January 1969, just a few days before he left office.

The campaign to get more American arms continued when Richard Nixon succeeded Johnson as president in 1969. Despite his characteristic bluntness, Rabin maintained good relations with many people in that administration, including Nixon himself, who was sympathetic toward Israel. It also helped that Nixon got along with Israeli Prime Minister Golda Meir, who succeeded Levi Eshkol at his death in early 1969. Also sympathetic was Joseph Sisco, a high State Department official, who appreciated that Rabin "says what he means and means what he says."[7] Rabin found additional support for Israel among leading Democrats such as Senators Henry Jackson of Washington and Stuart Symington of Missouri. He was especially fond of Jackson, an influential senator from a state with few Jewish voters, who stressed that "the American people support Israel."[8] Rabin said Jackson was "among my most—and Israel's most—cherished friends in the U.S. Senate."[9]

Rabin also developed an excellent relationship with Dr. Henry Kissinger, Nixon's national security advisor. Kissinger was a Jewish immigrant from Germany whose parents had fled the Nazis in the late 1930s. Many Israelis feared that precisely because he was Jewish, Kissinger would go overboard to prove his neutrality in the Arab-Israeli struggle, and therefore possibly favor the Arabs. Rabin found that not to be the case. With both Kissinger and Nixon, policy always was driven first and foremost by America's Cold War struggle with the Soviet Union, which included limiting Soviet influence in the Middle East. That required support for Israel, but also, Kissinger stressed to Rabin, strong U.S. ties with important Arab countries. Like Nixon, Kissinger was sympathetic toward Israel, but he was prepared to be very tough on Israel and pressure it to make concessions whenever it suited his overall Middle East strategy and American policy.

The two men developed a deep respect for one another. Rabin was extremely impressed by how Kissinger combined vast knowledge with a practical approach to problems, as well as the broad strategic

*Prime Minister Rabin and Secretary of State Henry Kissinger
had established a strong rapport ten years earlier when Rabin
was the Israeli Ambassador to the United States. Their
respect and admiration for each other's abilities seemed to be
on both a personal and political level.*

scope of his policies and diplomacy. Kissinger admired Rabin's integrity and noted that his "analytical brilliance in cutting to the core of a problem was awesome." Kissinger added, "I valued his judgment, often on matters unconnected with the Middle East."[10] However, neither man ever allowed personal respect to get in the way of national policy. Rabin experienced some of his most difficult moments in Washington, as well as some of his best, when dealing with Kissinger.

Rabin and Israel got much less sympathy from Nixon's secretary of state, William Rogers. Israel's ambassador also was confronted by the consistently pro-Arab outlook of several important officials within the State Department.

One problem that Rabin constantly faced was pressure from would-be mediators to get Israel to return all Arab land taken in 1967 before negotiations began. This was the approach of Gunnar Jarring, the UN diplomat in charge of promoting Arab-Israeli negotiations. Rabin, like most Israelis, had no faith in Jarring or in the UN, which Israelis believed had let them down time and again since independence. The numbers bear out Israeli suspicions. Between 1947 and 1989, the UN General Assembly passed 321 resolutions condemning Israel; the Security Council passed 49. During that period neither body passed a single resolution condemning any Arab state or the PLO. Rabin counted much more on the United States. That is why he was so disturbed when Secretary of State Rogers proposed his "Rogers Plan" in December 1969, which followed Jarring's approach. The Israeli government in Jerusalem and Rabin in Washington strongly criticized the plan, angering the Americans. However, the point became moot when the Egyptians also rejected the plan.

The Rogers Plan emerged during a tense period known as the "War of Attrition." In 1969, Egypt began bombarding Israeli positions on the east bank of the Suez Canal from its positions along the western bank. Its main goal was to cause as many Israeli casualties as possible and thereby force an Israeli withdrawal or other concessions. The fighting included continual hit-and-run attacks and aerial dogfights between warplanes. As their casualties mounted, Israel looked for ways to stop the Egyptian attacks.

Rabin recommended bombing raids on Egyptian military bases deep inside the country. Israel began these raids in January 1970, but the initial results were largely unfavorable. The Soviets responded by sending modern anti-aircraft missiles to Egypt, along with thousands of instructors and soldiers. Matters became worse when Soviet pilots began flying patrols near the Suez Canal and Soviet anti-aircraft missiles shot down several Israeli Phantoms. The tension came close to the boiling point on June 30, when Israeli fighters shot down four planes flown by Russian pilots. Both sides now drew back and a cease-fire took effect on August 7. Within days the Egyptians violated the cease-fire by moving Soviet anti-aircraft missiles up to the Suez Canal.

Within barely a month after the cease-fire a new Middle East crisis brought Israel and the United States closer than ever before. By 1970 the PLO had become so strong in Jordan that it threatened King Hussein's authority. In September, Hussein struck back furiously with his army to save his throne. In pitched battles thousands of Palestinians were killed. Some fled into Israel to escape the fury of the Jordanian wrath. The PLO itself relocated its headquarters to Lebanon. The Palestinians called this event "Black September." Meanwhile, to rescue the PLO, Syria sent 250 tanks across the Jordanian border. King Hussein suddenly had a far more serious threat on his hands.

At this point Rabin received an urgent call from Henry Kissinger. The United States was worried that if Syria toppled Hussein, Soviet influence in the Middle East would increase. Kissinger requested that Israel prepare to use its air force to save Hussein if that became necessary. Israel agreed, although it turned out that Jordan was able to drive the Syrian tanks back on its own. The entire matter was handled with great secrecy. Rabin used an obscure side entrance to the White House to avoid being seen when he delivered Israel's reply to Kissinger. This and other secret meetings with Kissinger led Rabin to observe:

> *In the course of scores of meetings with Kissinger,*
> *I must have become acquainted with every possible*
> *way of getting into the White House with the*
> *exception of sliding down the roof.*[11]

Israel came out of the crisis with new deals for additional American arms. They included Phantom and Skyhawk aircraft and modern M-60 tanks. The United States also increased its loans to Israel to help it pay for the expensive but vital new weapons. However, the flow of military technology was not all one way. For example, in 1969, Israeli forces along the Suez Canal captured an advanced Soviet radar station from the Egyptians. It was the same kind of radar being used in Vietnam to track and help shoot down American warplanes. The Israelis immediately sent the radar equipment to the United

States, so it could be studied and countermeasures developed to save the lives of American pilots.

Immediately after the Jordanian crisis, a new variable was thrown into the complex Middle East political equation. On September 28, 1970, Gamal Abdel Nasser, by far the Arab world's most important leader, suffered a heart attack and died. His successor was Egypt's little-known vice president, Anwar Sadat, whose policies were destined to surprise experts and politicians in capitals from Washington to Jerusalem to Moscow.

The Syrian-Jordanian confrontation was the last major crisis of Rabin's tenure in Washington. During the next two years, there were fruitless attempts to jump-start negotiations between Israel and Egypt. Both the Israeli government and Rabin himself have been criticized for missing a possible opportunity in 1971, when Egypt's President Sadat suggested reopening negotiations. In his memoirs, written after the fact, Rabin hints that he believed his government was being too rigid in responding to Sadat. In particular, Israel might have pulled back its troops a short distance from the Suez Canal to get negotiations started. He writes: "For a time I actually found myself in the rather unorthodox position of negotiating with my own government on a set of proposals for a partial agreement!"[12] In any event, 1971, which Sadat called the "year of decision," passed without any progress, as did 1972.

Still, the man who supposedly was "no diplomat" achieved a great deal as Israel's ambassador. Rabin was the first Israeli ambassador to Washington to gain access to the highest levels of the United States government on a regular basis. He played an important role in convincing the United States to sell Israel high-tech weapons.

He fostered ties between the Israeli and American military establishments. During his tenure, the United States came to view Israel as its only reliable partner in the Middle East.

Rabin also went beyond formal diplomacy. He reached out to non-Jewish audiences in the United States to present Israel's case. His varied contacts ranged from liberal labor leader George Meany to conservative religious leader Billy Graham. Rabin received invitations to lecture to groups all over the country and accepted as many as his schedule would allow.

The one arena where Rabin's outreach met difficulties was on the college campuses. Rabin understood that America's campuses were in turmoil because of opposition to the Vietnam War, but he was shocked and dismayed to find himself the target of extremist left-wing groups such as the Students for a Democratic Society and the Black Panthers. By the late 1960s they and similar radical groups were siding with the Arabs and viciously attacking Israel. When he spoke on college campuses Rabin was denounced as a murderer and worse. Tactics like heckling and fake bomb scares were used to disrupt his talks. Israel's ambassador was distressed that "in this greatest and proudest of democracies, young men and women were pouring so much energy into preventing a man from speaking his mind."

Even more painful was that in America's finest institutions of higher learning, "I was witnessing a self-righteous crusade based on sheer ignorance" of the history of Israel and the Jewish people. Rabin was especially disturbed because the accusation of "murderer" was "all too familiar in the annals of Jewish history." It was a "favorite anti-Semitic slander" used to turn people against the Jews "from the Dark Ages right through to modern times." Furthermore, "there was nothing new in turning on the Jews in times of crisis." Rabin wanted to tell his critics, "Read your history." But, as he wrote sadly in his memoirs, "they were too involved in their rage, and history was presumably irrelevant....They merely continued to hurl that age-old indictment at me in the ugly tradition of ignorance, prejudice, and hatred."[13]

In June 1972, Ambassador Rabin became embroiled in the upcoming American presidential election. While in Israel he indicated during a radio interview that he preferred the Republican candidate Richard Nixon to Democrat George McGovern. In truth, Rabin personally did prefer Nixon, since he thought McGovern's desire to cut the American defense budget and limit its worldwide commitments would hurt Israel. Rabin was accused of interfering in the American election. The *Washington Post* newspaper called him "Israel's undiplomatic diplomat." Rabin dismissed the charge by noting that the campaign had not yet begun and he was speaking to an Israeli audience that obviously was "not going to the [American] polls."[14]

Rabin's last day as ambassador was March 11, 1973. He was satisfied he had done his job well. As he left the United States he said, simply as usual but more diplomatically than usual, "I was happy to serve here and at the same time I'm happy to be going home."[15]

CHAPTER SIX

"The sons of the founding fathers have come of age."

W hen Rabin returned to Israel on March 11, 1973, he found a confident country. The economy was much stronger than in 1967. New immigrants in growing numbers were arriving from the Soviet Union, more than 30,000 in 1972 alone. Tens of thousands of new cars crowded Israel's narrow roads, while antennas sprouted like weeds to take advantage of television, introduced to the country after the Six-Day War. Israel's new borders, even if they were not permanent, at least appeared to give its people the safety they had never before enjoyed. Egypt's army was behind the Suez Canal, Syria's beyond the Golan Heights, and Jordan's across the Jordan River. Although tense, the borders were quiet. Like most Israelis, Rabin accepted the government's reassuring claim: "The lines are safe. The bridges are open. Jerusalem is united...and our political position is stable."[1] People were enjoying the peace; they gave little thought to war.

Rabin, at least personally, was a bit insecure; he was in the process of changing careers. After spending most of his adult life as a soldier, and then five years as a diplomat, he was about to enter the complex world of Israeli politics. Given his background as a socialist, it was natural that Rabin join Israel's political arena on the side of the Labor party, which was a combination of several socialist groups. Labor's main rival was Likud, a recently organized non-socialist party that itself was a combination of several political parties.

Under Israel's parliamentary system, voters traditionally cast their ballots for political parties rather than individuals. Each party received seats in the 120-member Knesset, or parliament, according to the percentage of votes it received. The seats were filled from a list that each party presented before the election, with the party leaders at the top of the list and lower-ranking members further down. The party with the most seats was then designated to form a government, and its leader became the country's prime minister. Israel also had a president, which was a largely ceremonial position.

This has always been a complicated process, because no single political party has yet succeeded in winning more than 50 percent of the vote in any parliamentary election. Forming a government, therefore, has always required a coalition of the victorious party with one or more smaller parties. In 1992 the electoral system was changed to allow direct election of the prime minister by the people.

Rabin clearly was popular with the Israeli public when he returned home, which is why the leaders of the

Labor party gave him the 20th place on their electoral list. Since the Labor party in its various forms had won every election in Israel's history, Rabin was assured a seat in the new Knesset.

By October the campaign was in full swing. Campaigning stopped for Yom Kippur, the Day of Atonement, the holiest day of the Jewish year. The holiday began at sundown on Friday, October 5, and lasted until sundown of October 6. But the election campaign would not begin again on October 7. On the afternoon of October 6, Egypt and Syria launched a massive air and ground attack on Israeli forces along the Suez Canal and on the Golan Heights. For the second time in barely six years, the Jewish state was fighting for its survival.

Unlike in 1967, Israel on Yom Kippur of 1973 was not prepared for war. The IDF had not taken into account the enormous amounts of ultramodern weapons, including antitank and anti-aircraft missiles, the Soviet Union had supplied to Egypt and Syria. Organization and discipline were not at the same high level as in 1967. Making matters worse, when the Israeli leadership finally realized on October 5 they were about to be attacked, they were unable, as in 1967, to strike first. If they did, the international community, swayed by its dependence on Arab oil, would come down very hard on Israel. The word from the United States, Israel's only reliable foreign friend, was blunt and unmistakable: "Don't preempt." In the tension-packed meetings just before the Egyptian/Syrian onslaught, Prime Minister Golda Meir and her cabinet rejected Chief of Staff David Elazar's urgent advice that Israel's air force attack the massing Arab troops. Meir explained her reasoning to the chief of staff in this way:

I know all the arguments in favor of a preemptive strike, but I am against it. We don't know, any of us, what the future will hold, but there is always the possibility that we will need help, and if we strike first, we will get nothing from anyone. I would like to say yes because I know what it would mean, but with a heavy heart I am going to say no.[2]

Israel and its soldiers paid a terrible price as a result.

As a retired general, Rabin found himself on the sidelines. He spent some time at the IDF headquarters in Tel Aviv at the start of the war, but did little as his successors ran the war. He accompanied Elazar on visits to the battlefront "and served as a sounding board whenever he asked me my opinion." Since he was not doing much, on the fourth day of the war he accepted an assignment to take charge of a war loan drive to raise money the government desperately needed. It was a task he "accepted without enthusiasm," but there was not much else he could do during this terrible time. As Rabin put it, during a war it "is difficult for a former chief of staff to put his mind to raising money."[3]

It took desperate fighting and extraordinary heroism to turn the tide of battle. The IDF's first priority was to stop the Syrians, whose advancing troops and tanks threatened to break into the Jordan Valley in northern Israel. In battles on the Golan Heights, Israeli tanks were outnumbered ten or twenty to one, and sometimes more. In one epic battle, the IDF's Seventh Armored Brigade, down to seven tanks from about one hundred, stopped a major Syrian advance. As the Syrians retreated on October 9, General Rafael ("Raful") Eitan, Israel's commander on the Golan, radioed a simple but chillingly accurate message to his exhausted men, "You have saved the people of Israel."[4]

Actually, more than two weeks of bitter fighting lay ahead. During the fighting the Soviet Union, which had encouraged Anwar Sadat and Syrian dictator Hafaz al-Assad to go to war, launched a huge airlift to resupply the Arab armies. A few days later, with Israel desperately short of weapons and ammunition, the United States began a massive airlift of its own that included everything from Phantom jets to artillery shells. However, not until the Israelis turned the tide of battle did the Soviet Union seek a cease-fire. The official cease-fire request came from United Nations Resolution 338, adopted on October 22, which also called for peace negotiations on the basis of UN Resolution 242. By then an Israeli army under General Ariel ("Arik") Sharon had fought its way across the Suez Canal, surrounding a major part of the Egyptian army. Three days later, with the Syrians routed, Egypt's army in a state of collapse, and Sadat in a state of panic, the shooting finally stopped.

Israel's price of victory in the Yom Kippur War was terrible. In a country of about 3 million, almost 3,000 soldiers were dead, the equivalent of almost 2.5 million dead for a country the size of the United States. Almost 9,000 soldiers were wounded. The war cost over $9 billion, more than Israel's entire gross national product for an entire year.

Israel, Egypt, and Syria were not the only countries to suffer from the war. Even as the fighting was going on, Saudi Arabia and other Arab oil producers declared a total oil embargo against the United States and several other countries for supporting Israel. The five-month-long oil boycott cost the United States 500,000 jobs and $10 to $20 billion in lost gross national product.

Still reeling from the war, Israelis went to the polls in December. Although Labor's strength declined, it remained the leading vote-getter. As Rabin recalled:

> *Considering they were exhausted, mourning their dead, and having difficulty digesting recent events or comprehending the significance of them, the voters were merciful to the Labor party.*[5]

However, the government formed by Golda Meir, which included Rabin as minister of labor, did not last long. There were angry protests against the leading figures in power before the war, especially Golda Meir and Defense Minister Moshe Dayan. In April a commission established to investigate Israel's failure to prepare for war issued its report. It put the blame on the military, especially Chief of Staff David Elazar. It was a conclusion that most citizens, Rabin included, did not accept. As Rabin saw it, "as soon as the government accepts the recommendations of the military, both share the consequences."[6] And that was the way it turned out. Elazar resigned, but the public uproar soon drove both Meir and Dayan into retirement. The Labor party had to find new leaders and organize a new government.

Although at first there appeared to be several candidates for the post of prime minister, the choice soon boiled down to Yitzhak Rabin and Shimon Peres. The contest was heated: According to Peres, the real origin of hostility between the two men was when "we ran against each other for the prime ministership and Labor party leadership in 1974."[7] Rabin was accused of profiting from his tour as Israeli ambassador by collecting $90,000 in lecture fees, a charge that fell flat when it was revealed that previous ambassadors had done the same thing. Far more serious, Ezer Weizman went public with the story of Rabin's emotional crises before the Six-Day War. Backed by strong support from Generals Sharon, Tal, and Yariv, Rabin survived that storm as well. In a close vote, on April 22, the Labor party's Central Committee selected him as party leader.

Now all Rabin had to do was form a government. That was not easy given the background of Labor's reduced strength in the Knesset and several intense personal rivalries within the Labor party leadership. At the same time, Rabin was involved in complicated and difficult negotiations to separate Israeli and Syrian forces on the Golan Heights. The negotiations were conducted by Henry Kissinger, who by now was the American secretary of state. In January 1974 he had come to the Middle East to arrange a separation of forces between Egyptian and Israeli troops in the Sinai. Because the Arabs would not meet the Israelis face to face, Kissinger "shuttled" between Cairo and Jerusalem until an agreement was reached. However, negotiations were more difficult with the Syrians, whose hatred of Israel was as strong as anywhere in the Arab world. Rabin had to twist his schedule to conform to Kissinger's as he conducted his "shuttle diplomacy" between Damascus and Jerusalem. "That left me little time for talks with possible coalition partners, though the construction of a government was not going to be a simple matter," Rabin remembered.[8]

Kissinger completed his mission successfully on May 31. On June 3, Rabin finally assembled his government. It had a precarious one-vote majority (61 seats) in the Knesset. The new government included Yigal Allon as foreign minister and deputy prime minister. Rabin yielded to political necessity—he had to take into account the Peres faction within the Labor party—and "with a heavy heart" appointed his rival to the post of defense minister.[9]

When Rabin became prime minister a new era began in Israel. Rabin was the first of his generation and the first native-born Israeli—or Sabra—to lead his country. As he put it in his acceptance speech to the Labor party leadership, "The sons of the founding fathers have come of age."[10] They had plenty of work ahead of them. The IDF had to be made more efficient and reinforced with new weapons. The new government also had to cope with economic problems caused by the war, and with a range of social problems as well.

Rabin decided he was strong enough to take several difficult but necessary economic steps after the National Religious party, with its ten seats in the Knesset, joined the government in October 1974. During 1974 and 1975 he reduced the government budget, devalued Israel's currency, and overhauled the tax system to cut loopholes and make it fairer. Determined to make the wealthy carry their share of the burden, he also banned imports of cars and other luxury products for six months. But Rabin's reforms could not prevent Israelis, with the country's huge defense budget, from being the highest-taxed people in the world. A wave of strikes and protests swept the country as Israel's working classes struggled to make ends meet.

On the security front, the Rabin government had to deal with growing terrorism by PLO groups. Just before Rabin became prime minister, two particularly vicious terrorist raids took place. On April 11, terrorists attacked the northern town of Kiryat Shmona and killed

18 people, including 8 children. An even worse attack took place on May 15 in the town of Ma'alot, where PLO terrorists seized a schoolhouse and held more than 100 children hostage. In the rescue attempt, 20 children died and 70 were wounded. More terrorist attacks followed, including one on July 4, 1975, in which a bomb hidden inside a refrigerator in downtown Jerusalem killed 14 and wounded 75 people.

With all this, and more, to deal with, Rabin's top priority was "to focus on moving away from war and toward some state of peace."[11] The separation of forces agreements of 1974 clearly were only temporary measures. They had to be reinforced and expanded to keep war from breaking out again. Rabin discussed both arms for the IDF and how to build on 1974 agreements with President Nixon during his June 1974 visit to Israel and during a meeting in the United States in September with Nixon's successor, Gerald Ford.

The meeting with Ford led to an unexpected crisis for which Rabin, usually a meticulous planner, was totally unprepared. At the conclusion of a state dinner, it was announced, to Rabin's dismay, that dancing would follow. Immediately, President Ford "bore down on Leah, bowed slightly, and swept her off to the brightly lit ballroom." Rabin was "on the spot."

> *If only I could dance—even poorly. If only someone would get in ahead of me and invite Mrs. Ford to the dance floor. But miracles of that nature do not happen at the White House. Deciding to adopt the tactics I followed in every sphere, I strode up to Mrs. Ford…swallowing hard, I explained, "I'm sorry, Mrs. Ford, but I simply don't know how to dance. Not a step."*

Rabin thought the "worst was over," until the smiling and gracious Mrs. Ford told him she had been a dance instructor as a young woman. Rabin found himself on the dance floor trying "to keep damage to a minimum." Finally Henry Kissinger "came to my rescue" and got Rabin off the dance floor. "If he had never done anything else for Israel, I would still be eternally grateful to Kissinger for that small mercy," Rabin remembered.[12]

Rabin soon was dealing with Kissinger on a more serious matter: maintaining the tenuous cease-fire in the Middle East. In March 1975, Kissinger arrived in the region for a new round of shuttle diplomacy. He did not find Rabin in a good mood. Just three days before Kissinger's arrival, a PLO terrorist attack on a seaside hotel in Tel Aviv had left eight Israelis dead. Rabin's angry response when he arrived at the scene was: "The only place we will meet the terrorists is on the battlefield."[13]

The talks bogged down immediately. Egypt demanded significant Israeli withdrawals in the Sinai that included the Abu Rudeis oil fields developed by Israel and the strategic Giddi and Mitla passes, the keys to the Sinai. In return, the Egyptians offered what Rabin considered only vague promises, what he told Kissinger were "words, words, words." Rabin could not convince Kissinger that his objections to the Egyptian terms were valid. Tempers rose and led to what Rabin called "the most painful conversation" the two men ever had.[14] Rabin was deeply concerned that the price of standing his ground would be high: a deterioration of Israeli-American relations. He was correct.

When the talks failed after ten days, President Ford announced a "reassessment" of American-Israeli relations. For six months the United States refused to sign new arms deals with Israel. Rabin worried not only about the arms but also how Israel's enemies would perceive and react to the apparent American-Israeli split. In September a new effort brought an agreement. Basically, a combination of Israeli concessions to American pressure and a complicated formula regarding control of the Mitla and Gidi passes broke the deadlock. Israel gave up the Abu Rudeis oil fields and retreated to the eastern end of the two passes. Egypt agreed to a pledge in which each side agreed not to "resort to the threat or use of force or military blockade" against the other.[15] The agreement was to last for three years. In letters from Ford and Kissinger to Rabin, the United States sweetened the deal by increasing both its arms supplies—including ultramodern F-16 fighter aircraft—and financial aid to Israel. The United States also agreed not to recognize the PLO unless it recognized Israel's right to exist and accepted UN Resolution 242. Rabin had succeeded in restoring American-Israeli relations to good health.

Despite Israel's improved relations with the United States, the Jewish state remained isolated in the international community. A combination of Arab oil money and Soviet-bloc influence had so biased the United Nations against Israel that it routinely and without cause passed anti-Israel resolutions. Some resolutions failed to be adopted only because the United States vetoed them in the Security Council. However, Israel's international standing improved briefly in mid-1976. The event responsible for this change took place not in the Middle East but in central Africa, at an airport in Uganda called Entebbe.

The chain of events that focused the world's attention on Entebbe began on June 27 when PLO terrorists hijacked an Air France aircraft just after it left Athens.

The flight had originated in Tel Aviv and was on its way to Paris. On board were 230 passengers, including 83 Israelis. The hijackers included Arabs and two Germans, a man and a woman. The plane ended up in Uganda, whose dictator, the notorious Idi Amin, collaborated with the hijackers. At that point the Israelis and other passengers with dual citizenship identified as Jews were separated from the other passengers. The hijackers demanded the release of over 50 terrorists imprisoned in several countries, including Israel. If their demands were not met, the hostages would be killed.

Israel had a policy of not negotiating with terrorists and using force to rescue hostages. But Entebbe was over 2,600 miles (4,100 kilometers) from Tel Aviv. In Jerusalem on June 29, Rabin asked Modechai Gur, the IDF chief of staff, if the military had a plan to rescue the hostages. Since at the time it did not, Rabin felt he had no choice but to negotiate, a decision on which he clashed with Defense Minister Shimon Peres, who opposed negotiations with terrorists regardless of the circumstances. As Rabin stalled for time with the terrorists, the IDF, pressed hard by Peres, worked furiously to come up with a workable plan.

Rabin was under enormous pressure. The families of the hostages, including one couple whom Leah knew personally, were demanding he make the terrorist/hostage exchange. He also knew a decision to launch a military rescue had to be made very soon, or it would be too late. Rabin stood his ground like a rock. He was well aware that whatever course he chose, he would "have to live with my conscience for the rest of my life." He did not want to give in to the terrorists, but, as always, he was unwilling to go ahead with a military operation until

*These passengers were just released from the hijacked
Air France Airbus. The Israeli and other Jewish passengers
who continued to be held hostage were rescued in a
spectacular operation which was approved by Rabin
only when he felt the preparations met the highest possible
standards. He himself estimated 15-20 would die during
the rescue, but agreed with the IDF chief of staff that
the operation was "the right thing to do."*

the preparations met the highest possible standards. He would not permit "a rescue operation with soldiers holding one-way tickets."[16]

The Israelis got a break when the terrorists made two errors. They extended their deadline until July 4, and they released their non-Jewish hostages. This gave the IDF more time. It also allowed Israeli intelligence officers to interview the former hostages and learn about the situation on the ground at Entebbe, such as the location of the captives, the hijackers, and Ugandan soldiers. On July 3, with time running out, Gur told the government that the IDF was ready. After being questioned by the cabinet about the risks, Gur said, "It's the right thing to do."[17] Fifteen minutes before the cabinet decided, four giant Hercules transport planes filled with equipment and Israeli paratroopers, and a Boeing 707 jet serving as the overall command plane, had taken off for Entebbe. The schedule was that tight. Had the cabinet voted no, the planes would have been recalled.

The overall commander of the operation was General Dan Shomron; he would be the first Israeli on the ground at Entebbe and the last to leave. The man in charge of the paratroopers assigned to liberate the hostages was Yonatan Netanyahu, a Harvard-educated officer and one of the IDF's outstanding soldiers. The operation was a stunning success. The lead Hercules landed undetected by flying in, according to plan, just behind a scheduled British flight. On the ground, surprise was maintained by hiding Israeli soldiers disguised as Ugandans inside a black Mercedes limousine and two jeeps, the exact vehicles Idi Amin used when he traveled. This allowed the paratroopers to reach the terminal where the hostages were being held without the hijackers knowing anything was happening. By then the paratroopers had removed their disguises—so they would not accidentally shoot at each other—and rushed into the terminal. The shooting inside the terminal lasted less than two minutes. Outside, another group of paratroopers destroyed eleven Ugandan military jet fighters on the ground to make sure they would not be used to shoot down any Israeli aircraft.

The first Hercules crammed with hostages took off 57 minutes after the first landing. The last Israeli aircraft followed 40 minutes later. Yet ultimate success did not prevent every one of those minutes from being harrowing. The last plane to leave just barely became airborne before reaching the end of a slick and muddy runway. Its pilot recalled his 90 minutes at Entebbe amid explosions and flying bullets, which at any moment could have disabled his plane:

> *I felt lonely and exposed, and each minute felt like a lifetime. It seemed a miracle that the preceding transports had escaped without incident. We planned a meticulous schedule. My head told me that everything was going according to plan, ticking like a well-oiled clock. But my belly told me: Everything can't be that perfect—you're the last one left.*[18]

Four hostages died at Entebbe, three at the airport and one who was in the hospital during the rescue and was later murdered by Ugandan soldiers. The rest were returned safely to Israel. All six hijackers guarding the hostages were killed. Israel suffered one military death when Netanyahu was shot in the back. In honor of the young hero the country affectionately called Yoni, Israelis named the Entebbe mission Operation Yonatan. Rabin personally felt each loss and wrote, "There can be no consolation for the bereaved families." Yet, he added, the losses were "smaller than I dared to hope."[19]

The success at Entebbe brought overwhelming joy to Israel. It boosted the country's confidence, still shaken by the Yom Kippur War. Entebbe also boosted Rabin's political standing when he needed it. Further afield, people all over the world reacted with enthusiasm and admiration for Israel, the only country that seemed willing or able to deal with the growing problem of international terrorism. And for a while, foreign governments seemed to have learned something; in several cases during the following few years they successfully used police or special antiterrorist units to end hijackings or hostage-taking incidents.

One of the most complex problems that Rabin faced as prime minister was how to deal with the territories conquered during the Six-Day War. Rabin always believed that Israel should be prepared to return territory for peace. At the same time, he was convinced that Israel could not go back to its dangerous 1967 borders. They had left the country with a narrow 9-mile (14-kilometer) waist near Tel Aviv, put its northern settlements under Syrian guns, and left Israeli towns near the Mediterranean coast only minutes away from the Egyptian army in the Gaza Strip. Israel had to retain some of the conquered territory in order to protect its security.

Aside from Jerusalem and its environs, Rabin believed that Israel had to hold part of the Golan Heights and certain parts of the West Bank, especially the thinly settled Jordan Valley. Here, Rabin and Labor disagreed with Menachem Begin and Likud, who opposed giving up any part of the West Bank, an area they referred to by its Biblical names of Judea (the southern part) and Samaria (the northern part). Rabin also believed that Israel's security required control of the Gaza Strip and Sharm el-Sheikh in the Sinai Peninsula. He did not want Israel to keep areas heavily populated by Arabs. Overall, his ideas were close to a 1967 proposal of his old mentor Yigal Allon, appropriately called the Allon Plan.

Rabin also agreed with most Israelis that under no circumstances should an independent Palestinian state be established on the Gaza Strip and West Bank. Such a state, they were convinced, would not be satisfied with anything less than the destruction of Israel. In any event, it would not solve the Arab-Israeli conflict. The core of that conflict, Rabin pointed out, was the refusal of all the Arab states to recognize Israel's right to exist. Under Rabin, Israel continued to refuse to recognize the PLO, which in any event also refused to recognize Israel's right to exist. He tried to reach an agreement with Jordan about how to divide the West Bank, and met secretly with King Hussein five times. Those meetings did not produce any results.

In the territories themselves, Rabin continued the policy of establishing and expanding Jewish settlements in strategically important areas away from centers of Arab population. These settlements were in the Jordan Valley, in parts of the Gaza Strip, and on the Golan Heights. However, the government was under pressure from certain religious and militant groups to place Jewish settlements in areas associated with ancient Jewish history and the Bible. The trouble was that most of these areas were centers of Arab population, such as the town of Hebron, where the patriarch Abraham, father of the Jewish people, is believed by many to be buried.

The best organized of the groups pressing for settlements in Biblical areas was called Gush Emunim (Community of the Believers). Its strategy was to begin settlements without government permission and exploit divisions within Israeli society and even within Rabin's cabinet to keep the government from evicting them. Between 1974 and 1977, the group was able to establish five settlements on the West Bank outside government-approved areas, including the town of Kiryat Arba near Hebron. The Likud party strongly supported these efforts.

By 1977 the ground was beginning to move under Rabin's feet. The United States had a new president, Jimmy Carter, about whom Rabin felt very uneasy. While visiting Washington in March, he was stunned when Carter told a press conference that Israel should withdraw to its 1967 borders, with slight modifications. Meanwhile, there were major problems at home. There was constant tension between Rabin and Peres. As Rabin put it, "It was no secret that there was a considerable degree of friction between the defense minister and myself."[20] In fact, in February, Peres challenged Rabin for the post of Labor party leader, losing in the party's Central Committee by a small margin.

The victory did Rabin little good. In mid-March, a story broke in the Israeli press that Mrs. Rabin had kept a bank account in the United States after Rabin's term as ambassador to the United States ended. Then it turned out that there were two accounts. Keeping such a foreign account was illegal under Israeli law at the time. Although most Israelis did not consider the offense to be a major one, the news was embarrassing, especially since

In 1977, the Likud party won the election and Begin became Prime Minister. The old hard-line politician then revealed surprising flexibility which enabled him to reach a point where successful negotiations with Anwar Sadat were possible. This photograph shows a remarkable moment in the history of Israel—Prime Minister Begin welcomes Egyptian President Anwar Sadat to Israel.

it came on the heels of several financial scandals involving other Labor politicians.

Rabin was adamant that he would share responsibility for the account with Leah. He decided he had no choice but to resign his office. Eventually a court fined Leah the huge amount of $27,000 (more money than was in the two accounts) for her violation of the law (which was later repealed). Yitzhak was fined a lesser amount ($1,600), because his name technically appeared on the accounts Leah had managed. Despite public sympathy, he was leaving office under a cloud.

Labor's fortunes also declined. In elections in May 1977, the Likud scored an enormous upset. Led by Menachem Begin, it soundly defeated Labor led by Peres. Israel not only would have a new prime minister, but for the first time since the founding of the state a new party would be in power. For Israel, and for Yitzhak Rabin, a new era had begun.

CHAPTER SEVEN

"Yet he strode like a soldier...."

Between June 1977 and June 1984, Israel was governed by a coalition led by the Likud party. For most of that period the country's prime minister was Menachem Begin. Born in Poland, Begin belonged to the generation that had founded Israel. Most of his family had died in the Holocaust. He arrived in Palestine in 1942, after a harrowing roundabout journey that initially took him from Poland to a Soviet prison camp in Siberia. Begin then became the fiery underground leader of the Irgun in the struggle against the British prior to 1948. He was the leading opposition politician during the next 29 years when Labor governments ruled the country. After Begin retired from public life in 1983, Yitzhak Shamir, likewise a veteran underground leader born in Poland, took his place as Likud's leader and Israel's prime minister.

The Likud years were filled with important events, including Anwar Sadat's dramatic visit to Jerusalem in

1977 and Israel's momentous peace treaty with Egypt in 1979, the first ever with an Arab state. Yet, like Peres and the rest of the Labor leadership, Rabin had to view these historic events from the sidelines as a member of the main opposition party in the Knesset. Leah Rabin summed up her husband's mood during what may be considered the Begin era:

> *He didn't enjoy those years from 1977 to 1984.*
> *He was bored to tears. He would call me three*
> *or four times a day, sometimes out of frustra-*
> *tion and boredom. There was no action. He's*
> *basically a doer. He likes responsibility. But*
> *he didn't consider doing anything else outside*
> *of politics.*[1]

By far the most important development that Rabin watched from the sidelines was the 1979 peace treaty. Menachem Begin and Anwar Sadat, the two men most responsible for making it happen, were unlikely partners. Begin was known as an unyielding hard-liner when dealing with the Arabs; Sadat's background included being imprisoned by the British during World War II for his pro-Nazi sympathies. Yet by 1977 both men believed that they had to leave at least part of the past behind. Sadat's own mistrust of Israel was reduced in mid-1977 when the Israelis warned him of an assassination plot against him, complete with names and addresses of the Palestinian assassins already in Cairo.

The first step had to come from Sadat, since for decades Egypt had refused to negotiate directly with Israel. On November 9, 1977, he told the Egyptian parliament that he was ready "to go to their own house, to the

Knesset" to talk to the Israelis.[2] Ten days later Sadat walked off an airplane at Israel's Ben-Gurion Airport. Rabin watched the "uniquely electric moment" from his place in the receiving line. He was impressed by how Sadat, "meeting all his former archenemies, one after another, in the space of seconds," somehow knew "exactly the right thing to say to each and every one of them."[3] Rabin also was impressed by Sadat's speech to the Knesset the next day, especially when he told the Israelis that he understood their need for security. As Rabin noted with some irony, "It was a statement we had never heard before—even from some of Israel's best friends."[4]

Yet long and difficult negotiations lay ahead. Finally, in September 1978, President Carter brought Begin and Sadat together in the United States where the three leaders hammered out a preliminary agreement called the Camp David Accords. The accords had two "frameworks." The first called for Israel, Egypt, Jordan, and undefined "representatives of the Palestinian people" to negotiate terms for limited Palestinian self-government in the West Bank and Gaza. It called for a five-year transition period, during which the parties would negotiate the final status of those territories. In effect, the Palestinian issue was put off so that Israel and Egypt could agree on the second "framework" dealing with a peace treaty between their two countries. On September 25, Rabin spoke in favor of the accords in the Knesset and joined an overwhelming majority of that body in approving them after an intense debate.

After more hard negotiations, an Israeli-Egyptian peace treaty was signed at the White House on March 26, 1979. At Begin's invitation, a pleased Yitzhak Rabin was present at the ceremony. Although Rabin had no role in the peace negotiations, he was convinced that his 1975 agreement with Egypt as well as later efforts until 1977 helped pave the way for the treaty signed in 1979. As he put it:

> *Mr. Begin was kind enough to invite me as a former prime minister and, I like to believe, in recognition of my contribution in paving the way for the final peace process.*[5]

The peace with Egypt came at a high price for Israel. Israel gave up the entire Sinai Peninsula, including Sharm el-Sheikh. Israel lost its important military bases in the Sinai, in which it had invested $10 billion. The cost of moving and building new bases was over $4 billion, only a quarter of which was covered by American aid. Additional billions invested in developing oil wells in the Sinai, which in 1979 were providing half of Israel's energy needs, also were forfeited. Begin also agreed to remove all Jewish settlements in the region, including the seaside town of Yamit, where he had hoped someday to retire. In return, Egypt accepted strict limits on the troops and weapons it could keep in the Sinai; in effect, a large part of the peninsula became a buffer zone between Israel and Egypt. Egypt pledged to allow Israeli ships through the Straits of Tiran and, for the first time, through the Suez Canal. Each side accepted the other's right to live at peace with "secure and recognized boundaries" and agreed to establish normal diplomatic, economic, and cultural ties.

In Israel the peace treaty was greeted with enthusiasm, although also with considerable caution. A minority opposed the agreement, mainly on security grounds.

While those fears proved to be unfounded, the treaty certainly did not produce the people-to-people ties that Israelis had wanted. The Egyptian government kept its relations with Israel strictly formal. There were few cultural or economic ties, and popular hostility to Israel among the Egyptian people remained intense and widespread. Borrowing from the language of the Cold War, Israelis referred to their relationship with Egypt as a "Cold Peace."

The Arab world outside of Egypt, from the PLO to the other Arab states, reacted to the peace treaty with fury. Within five days, nineteen of the Arab League's twenty-two members met in Baghdad, Iraq, and announced a series of sanctions against Egypt. Over the next two months most Arab countries broke diplomatic relations with Egypt. Egypt was suspended from the Arab League, expelled from the Islamic Conference, and thrown out of several other international Arab organizations. Two years later, Sadat was assassinated by Muslim extremists opposed to any peace with Israel.

Although the state of war between Israel and Egypt ended, the feud between Yitzhak Rabin and Shimon Peres continued. It was fueled by both political differences and personal rivalry. In the 1960s the two men had disagreed on several policy issues. In the 1970s two ambitious and highly capable men with very different styles—Rabin, the ex-general, direct and blunt; Peres, the intellectual career politician, smooth and subtle—were competing for their party's leadership and the country's top post. Not surprisingly, the feud did neither man any good and often angered other party leaders, who saw that the Rabin-Peres infighting was damaging Labor's chances to unseat Likud. Many of those leaders were especially upset by

Rabin's strident attacks on Peres in *The Rabin Memoirs*, published in 1979. It seemed hard to believe that the Peres pictured by Rabin was the same man who for many years had played such a critical role in developing Israel's defense capabilities and its nuclear research program. Rabin's use of his memoirs to attack Peres was not his finest hour. If anything, it undermined his position in the party. When he challenged Peres for the party leadership in December 1980, Rabin was soundly defeated. Peres received an overwhelming 70 percent of the Central Committee's votes.

Peres therefore led Labor in the 1981 campaign leading up to the elections on June 30. Likud actually struck its most powerful blow in the campaign 500 miles (800 kilometers) from Israel. On June 7, eight American-built F-16 fighter-bombers destroyed Iraq's Osiraq nuclear reactor, which was still under construction. It was a feat that rivaled the Entebbe mission. The planes had to fly to the very limit of their range over Jordanian and Saudi Arabian territory and take special precautions to avoid being detected by radar. The pilots then bombed their target with what one observer called "stupefying accuracy."[6] Begin had throttled the Iraqi nuclear weapons program. At the time, Israel was severely criticized by the international community, including the United States. Ten years later, when Americans and other soldiers faced the Iraqi army in Kuwait during operation Desert Storm, that criticism turned to belated praise.

Rabin supported the raid, saying "everything should be done" to postpone or prevent an Arab state from getting nuclear weapons.[7] The Israeli voters showed their support at the polls. Likud came from behind in the polls to narrowly win the election. Begin then put together a new Likud-led coalition government to govern the country for the next four years.

Begin was much less successful in another bold strike closer to home. In 1982, Israel invaded Lebanon. Lebanon was a weak and unstable country, divided into a variety of feuding Muslim and Christian groups. It was about half Christian, making it unique in the almost totally Muslim Arab world. For that reason, Israeli leaders thought it might be possible to make peace with Lebanon, despite its many internal divisions, if they could help the local Christians consolidate their power. As prime minister, Rabin also tried to play the Lebanon card. On one occasion he secretly sailed northward in a navy gunboat and met with the leader of one of the local Christian factions just off the Lebanese coast.

Since 1970 the PLO had built up a powerful presence in Lebanon, a veritable "state within a state." Southern Lebanon became a PLO base for attacking Israel. During 1981, PLO rocket attacks on settlements in northern Israel brought civilian activity in several areas to a halt. Begin was persuaded to invade Lebanon by Ariel Sharon, his new defense minister. The stated goal of the invasion was to drive the PLO from southern Lebanon and restore security to northern Israel. However, under Sharon's direction the invasion soon took on greater scope, as Israeli troops advanced to Beirut, Lebanon's capital. Sharon intended to drive the PLO from the country entirely, force Syrian forces out as well, and help create a Christian-dominated Lebanese government that would make peace with Israel.

At first Rabin supported both the invasion and Sharon. He even supported the IDF's siege of Beirut and visited the defense minister at the front lines several times. But Rabin became concerned as the invasion turned into an occupation. He doubted Israel's expanded goals in Lebanon could be achieved and, like other Israelis, was appalled at the IDF's mounting casualties. In 1983, Rabin warned against Israel getting stuck in the *botz ha'Levanoni*, or the Lebanese mud. As it turned out, he soon would be given the difficult job of getting Israel out of that mud.

In August 1983, Menachem Begin suddenly retired from public life. He gave no reason, but it appeared that the recent death of his wife and the growing cost of the fighting in Lebanon had taken their toll on him. Begin was succeeded by sixty-eight-year-old Yitzhak Shamir, a hard-liner who had opposed returning Sinai to Egypt. In June 1984, Israelis once again went to the polls. Their concern with losses in Lebanon, mounting inflation and other economic problems, and squabbling politicians showed in the election results. Both Labor and Likud lost strength, the former winning forty-four seats and the latter forty-one.

The result, after several months of political maneuvering, was a National Unity Government organized in September. The parties would share power according to a "rotation" plan. For the first two years Peres would be prime minister and Shamir foreign minister. Then they would switch posts. The two parties agreed that the other key post, defense minister, would be filled for the full four-year term by one man: Yitzhak Rabin. After seven years in the political wilderness, Rabin had returned to power. Leah Rabin was flushed with pride and joy for her husband:

Seventeen years after removing his uniform,
Yitzhak had returned to the defense establishment
as though coming home after a prolonged absence,
full of ups and downs in life. Seventeen years had
passed, his hair had turned grey and he was
wearing a suit in place of a uniform. Yet he strode
like a soldier, as in the past, his face not revealing
his inner feelings.[8]

Rabin's first task in his new post was to get the IDF out of Lebanon. This was urgent given the growing cost in Israeli lives, which passed 500 even before Rabin took office. One of the worst incidents took place just after Rabin became minister of defense. In November 1983, a booby-trapped truck blew up at an Israeli military checkpoint. It killed 29 soldiers and wounded many more. Debates within the government about how fast to withdraw took place during 1984. As frequently was the case, Rabin and Peres disagreed, Peres supporting an immediate full withdrawal and Rabin favoring one in stages. By then Israel's main goal was reduced to maintaining a security zone along the border free of both the PLO and the Syrians. What happened in the rest of Lebanon, Israel could not control. As Rabin told the American press, "I don't want to be the policeman of Lebanon."[9]

The withdrawal took place in stages as Rabin wanted and was completed by June 1985. Israel kept a small contingent of soldiers in Lebanon in a narrow "security zone" along Israel's northern border. It also backed a small militia of Lebanese Christians that operated in the zone to protect local Christian villages from the PLO and other armed Muslim groups. The Begin-Sharon invasion had destroyed the PLO's state-within-a-state in Lebanon. But the cost in lives and morale was terribly high, and the enterprise had not achieved any of Sharon's other goals or left Israel in a position to prevent the subsequent return of armed PLO forces to Lebanon.

Rabin's great challenge as minister of defense did not come from abroad. It came from an uprising that began in December 1987 in the Gaza Strip and quickly spread to the West Bank. Soon it took on a life and intensity that nobody expected. It would last almost six years and is known as the Intifada, an Arabic term that means "shaking off." The Intifada reflected the deep frustration and despair among Palestinians in the territories who lived under Israeli rule, especially young people who had been born and grown up under Israeli occupation. They hated the Israelis, but also felt deserted by the rest of the Arab world.

As minister of defense, Rabin was the man on the spot whose job was to stop the Intifada. He was in the United States at the time of the first riots and did not return home until the Intifada was two weeks old. Rabin therefore has been accused by Israelis of not recognizing quickly enough that something unprecedented in scope had broken out. If the criticism is valid, and it would seem to be, then Rabin was hardly the only person who should have been more in touch with the mood of Palestinians in the territories. From his headquarters in Tunisia, PLO chairman Yasir Arafat also mistakenly viewed the December rioting as something that he had seen before and would pass. That is why he described the incidents with the word "intifada," which in the past Arabs had applied to relatively limited outbursts.

The Intifada spread like wildfire and defied Rabin's attempts to control it. There were constant riots and attacks on Israeli settlers and soldiers. Israeli settlers were a prime target in part because after 1977 the Likud government had followed a policy of building new Jewish settlements anywhere on the West Bank, including areas near large Arab population centers. The attacks could be deadly, as the rioters not only threw stones but also gasoline-filled bottles called Molotov cocktails. When Israeli troops used force to quell the riots, people, often teenagers, were killed. The riots and the Israeli response was filmed by the press and watched by millions of people throughout the world. The news coverage created a public-relations disaster for the Jewish state. Foreign television viewers usually were not aware that the PLO soon took control of many Intifada actions and used them for its own purposes. Nor did foreign viewers in Europe and the United States understand that Intifada activists had become skilled at manipulating and intimidating the foreign press to get the coverage they wanted.

Rabin's hard-line policy against the Intifada was called the "iron fist," a term that did little to improve Israel's public image. Even his attempts to reduce Palestinian casualties backfired. IDF troops were issued clubs and told to use them instead of firing their rifles whenever possible. As a result, the world saw television pictures of Israeli troops beating Palestinian youths, making Israel look even worse. Rabin admitted that he was "surprised to discover that the sensitivity of world opinion to blows and physical confrontation was greater than to that of shooting."[10]

During the first year of the Intifada, more than 150 Palestinians were killed and 11,500 were wounded. Part of the Israeli dilemma was summed up by General Dan Shomron, the leader of the Entebbe raid and the current IDF chief of staff:

> *People are constantly pressuring us to come down hard [on the Palestinians]. But I'm also thinking about the future, about the question of who will have to live here, and I'm trying not to burn our bridges.*[11]

As for Rabin, within a few months he admitted, "It is far easier to solve classic military problems" than to quell a mass uprising.[12]

The Intifada dragged on into the 1990s. Neither side was able get its way, and both sides were seeing consequences they did not like. The death toll, among both Palestinians and Israelis, was mounting. Within the Palestinian community, the constant closing of schools was depriving a generation of education. There was a general rise of lawlessness, as extremist elements and criminals used the cover of the uprising to take revenge on their opponents or rivals. It was enough to label someone an "Israeli collaborator," regardless of the facts, to put his life in grave danger. During 1992 and 1993, more Palestinians were killed by other Palestinians, often with great cruelty, than by Israeli troops. Meanwhile, Palestinian leaders could see that Israel was not disappearing, and was in fact growing stronger and larger as hundreds of thousands of immigrants continued to arrive, recently having been allowed to leave the Soviet Union and its successor states.

Nor could the Israelis find comfort in their frustrating struggle against the Intifada. Many Israelis were deeply troubled by the harsh measures that the IDF had to use to control Palestinian rioters. Parents who were prepared to see their sons at risk on a battlefield did not want them swinging clubs against teenagers in the territories. Meanwhile, the Intifida was undermining the morale of the IDF, which was supposed to defend the country against foreign armies, not chase gangs of youths in the streets and alleys of cities and towns. Time spent on the West Bank also took away from training exercises vital to battle readiness. Still another problem was that the Intifada boosted the influence of a fundamentalist Islamic organization called Hamas, which was more extreme than most of the factions in the PLO. Hamas rejected any thought of negotiations of peace with Israel or with Jews, whom Hamas called "the sons of monkeys and swines."[13]

As Israelis looked for a way out of the quagmire, some of them began to change their attitude toward the Palestinians. One person whose thinking was evolving was Yitzhak Rabin. Ironically, the Intifada improved his standing among the Israeli public, which generally saw him as a tough and uncomplaining soldier willing to take the heat to protect them. A poll in March 1988 showed Rabin more popular than either Peres or Shamir. Yet Rabin was becoming convinced that Israel could not continue to rule over a large and hostile Arab population. The use of force against the Intifada had reached a dead end. Only a political solution could end the violence. During the spring of 1988 and into 1989, in search of new ideas, he met secretly with Palestinian notables from the West Bank. Those discussions produced no concrete results, however.

In November 1988, national elections produced another virtual dead heat between Likud and Labor, with Likud edging out its rival by one seat, 40 to 39. Once again, the two parties formed a national-unity government with Shamir as prime minister. However, by 1990 the tension within the government had reached the breaking point over a new American peace initiative. The United States under President George Bush wanted to set up a peace conference that would include a delegation of Palestinian Arabs unaffiliated with the PLO. Shamir took a hard line on exactly which non-PLO Palestinians would be acceptable to Israel. Peres and his supporters within Labor wanted Israel to be more flexible. They accused Shamir of subverting the peace process, and he retorted that they were prepared to make unwise concessions. These differences were piled on top of the Labor-Likud disagreement about whether Israel should give up land for peace, which Labor favored and Likud opposed. Rabin, who had his problems with both Shamir and Peres, finally decided Shamir's stalling was unacceptable. With its two normally quarreling leaders in agreement, Labor quit the unity government, thereby bringing it down.

The next few months saw a swirl of political squabbling. Peres, as party leader, failed in his attempt to form a Labor government. For Peres, losing the chance to become prime minister was a deep personal disappointment and a severe political setback. Shamir then succeeded in getting several religious parties to join a Likud-led coalition. The Israeli public as a whole reacted angrily to the political wheeling and dealing it took to form a government. There were widespread demands for electoral reform that would reduce the influence of small political parties and strengthen the political center.

Rabin meanwhile took advantage of Peres's failure to challenge him for the Labor leadership. This time it was Rabin's turn to be disappointed. Although Rabin seemed to be the most popular politician in the country, Peres still held sway inside Labor's Central Committee. In July it again chose him over Rabin. However, Labor was listening to the popular outcry. Once the 1990 leadership battle was over, the committee voted to change its election system. Instead of the Central Committee deciding the matter, the party would hold an American-style primary and allow the membership to choose its leader.

In August 1990, one month after Rabin's unsuccessful challenge to Peres, almost everything in the Middle East was put on hold when Iraqi dictator Saddam Hussein invaded neighboring Kuwait. By seizing Kuwait and adding its vast oil reserves to those of Iraq, Hussein suddenly had control of almost 20 percent of the world's total supply. And next door for the taking was Saudi Arabia, with a quarter of the world's oil. The United States responded by forming a coalition of countries from around the world, including Egypt and Saudi Arabia, that drove Iraq from Kuwait in January 1991.

Israel's role, which it accepted reluctantly, was to stay out of the action and not retaliate against Iraqi missile attacks (using Soviet Scud missiles) on its cities. If Israel defended itself, the United States feared, the Arab states would defect from the coalition. After the war, when the full extent of Iraq's nuclear weapons and poison-gas programs became known, the wisdom of Israel's 1981 attack against Iraq's nuclear reactor received far greater recognition. A major loser in the Gulf War, aside from Iraq, was the PLO, which strongly supported the invasion of Kuwait and the missile attacks against Israel.

In the aftermath of the Gulf War the United States put new pressure on the Shamir government to come to a peace conference. The result was the Madrid Conference, which began on October 30, and was co-sponsored by the United States and the Soviet Union. It gave Israel a chance to negotiate directly with Lebanon, Jordan, and Syria on the basis of UN resolutions 242 and 338. The Palestinians were represented as part of a joint Jordanian-Palestinian delegation. This reflected Israel's steadfast refusal to negotiate with the PLO, whose covenant still called for Israel's destruction. Although the Madrid Conference yielded little concrete progress, in retrospect it was a step forward. For the first time, Israel was negotiating face-to-face with its front-line Arab adversaries: Syria, Lebanon, and a joint Jordanian-Palestinian delegation.

Back in Israel, Shamir's participation at Madrid appeared to be winning increased public support for Likud. The party looked to be in better shape than Labor for the coming elections in June. But the political ground was shifting fast in Israel. By the time it stopped moving, Labor would win a solid victory and Yitzhak Rabin would reclaim the office of prime minister.

CHAPTER EIGHT

"We must take risks."

It took two changes in Israel's political alignment to bring Yitzhak Rabin to power as prime minister. First, Rabin had to capture the Labor party leadership from Peres; second, Labor had to defeat Likud in a general election.

The first change occurred when Labor selected its new leader and candidate for prime minister in Israel's first-ever primary election in February 1992. Two other candidates joined the perennial rivals Rabin and Peres in the primary. Labor's rules required that the winning candidate get over 40 percent of the vote. Otherwise, the two candidates with the most votes would compete in a runoff.

The primary took place on February 19. Rabin was cautiously optimistic, but hardly overconfident in a race that most people correctly rated a toss-up between him and Peres. As Leah recalled, Rabin "was under control.

I was going out of my mind."[1] When the ballots were counted, Rabin received 40.59 percent of the vote. It was not an overwhelming victory, but it was enough.

While Rabin was grasping the reigns of power inside the Labor party, Likud was losing its power in the country as a whole. A number of factors undermined the Shamir government. While it continued to invest huge sums in Jewish settlements on the West Bank, Shamir's government neglected the parts of Israel inside the 1967 borders where most of its citizens (over 96 percent) lived. By the spring of 1992 unemployment approached 12 percent, never a good sign for the future of any democratically elected government. Among the new immigrants, including the hundreds of thousands from the former Soviet Union, unemployment was a staggering 40 percent.

Shamir's refusal to slow down the settlement program on the West Bank or consider territorial compromise in negotiations with the Arabs strained relations with the United States, a development that worried Rabin as well as most Israelis. Following Begin's approach, the most that Shamir was willing to offer the Palestinians was local autonomy in their cities and towns; Israel would retain physical control of the region. By 1992, Shamir's hard line was losing its appeal at home, mainly because the public was weary of the unending stalemate. Israelis increasingly seemed to feel that Israel could do more to move peace negotiations forward without endangering its security.

Shamir's government collapsed in January 1992 when two small rightist parties walked out of the Likud-led coalition. As Likud entered the election campaign that followed, it was plagued by internal conflict between factions respectively led by Housing Minister Sharon, Foreign Minister David Levy, and Shamir. Meanwhile, Labor managed temporarily to circumvent its internal quarrels, including the usual Rabin-Peres tension, and unite behind Rabin.

A key factor in Rabin's victory over Peres in the Labor primary was that many party members believed that their best chance in the general election was with Rabin at the head of the ticket. The party's campaign reflected that sentiment. Labor muted its traditional socialist identity and went to the people as "Labor headed by Rabin." Instead of its trademark socialist red flag, the party shifted to blue, which is identified with Israel's blue-and-white flag and therefore with nationalist feelings. The main campaign slogans ran: "Israel is waiting for Rabin" and "Rabin is the only hope."[2]

Rabin meanwhile promised a new orientation. He said that a Labor government would no longer sink money into any and all settlements on the West Bank, many of which, he insisted, did nothing for Israel's security. Rather, his government would shift priorities from the territories to Israel proper, where, he charged, Likud's neglect had left everything from roads to schools to social programs in disrepair. As for peace negotiations, still the key issue, he pledged a new and more flexible effort to reach agreements with the Palestinians as well as with Jordan and Syria.

Rabin's reputation as Israel's "Mr. Security," earned from his military career and years as minister of defense fighting the Intifada, was crucial to Labor's chances in the election. That reputation counterbalanced the general public's view of Labor as dominated by leftist and dovish politicians, many associated with Peres, who would give away too much and compromise Israel's security in negotiations with the Arabs. Rabin's reputation allowed him to stake out a position that appeared to promise both flexibility and security. As he wrote on June 1, 1992, in an Israeli newspaper:

> *I am unwilling to give up a single inch of Israel's security, but I am willing to give up many inches of sentiments and territories—as well as 1,700,000 Arab inhabitants—for the sake of peace. That is the whole doctrine in a nutshell. We seek a territorial compromise which will bring peace and security. A lot of security.*[3]

Rabin stressed that "a lot of security" meant retaining territory around Jerusalem, the Jordan Valley south of Lake Kinneret, and the Golan Heights. On the other hand, it also meant that Israel could not continue to rule over 1.7 million hostile Arabs in the territories. In saying that, Rabin still firmly opposed an independent Palestinian state on the West Bank and Gaza. A Palestinian state, he warned, inevitably would fall under control of radical forces who would not be satisfied until they destroyed Israel. Any territories that Israel gave up would have to return to Jordanian control in one way or another. In a televised debate with Shamir a week before the election on June 23, Rabin summed up the "three points on which I will stand: no Palestinian state; no return to the 1967 borders; and a united Jerusalem under Israeli control."[4]

Labor's strategy paid off. With Rabin leading the charge, it defeated Likud by the decisive margin of 44 seats to 32. Actually, the large margin was due far more to Likud's losses (it fell from 40 to 32 seats) than Labor's gains (from 39 to 44). After fifteen years, Yitzhak Rabin once again was charged with putting together a coalition to govern Israel.

The job of assembling a coalition was easier than in 1977, mainly because of two new political parties. One was called Meretz. It was formed in 1992 when three small parties on the left that shared dovish views regarding negotiations with the Arabs merged. Meretz was eager to add its 12 seats to Labor's 44. Six more seats, putting Labor over the threshold of 60, came from a religious party called Shas, formed in 1984.

Rabin's goal, however, was to form a centrist coalition that could claim support across a wide arc of Israel's spectrum. During the election he had promised that his government would not tilt to the left or right. To keep that promise Rabin had to balance Meretz. The only available ballast on the right was yet another new party, called Tsomet, formed in 1988. It was led by Raphael Eitan, a former general and one of the heroes of the Yom Kippur War and a hard-liner on how to deal with the West Bank and Gaza. But efforts to bring Tsomet into Rabin's coalition failed, leaving Rabin with a government whose tilt away from the center of Israeli politics was deepened by a tactical alliance with five Arab members of the Knesset. Although not officially members of the government, they consistently sided with it in Knesset votes.

In his new government Rabin took on the post of defense minister as well as prime minister. Peres became foreign minister, a position that Rabin had to give his old rival because of his strong following in the Labor party. During the campaign, relations between the two men, as Peres put it, "were strained." After the election they met privately to establish a working relationship. Rabin already had made it clear that he intended to be in charge, a situation that Peres, swallowing his pride, had to accept. Yet both men were determined to subordinate everything, including their personal rivalry, to the greater goal of making peace. On that basis, and with time slowly healing old wounds, Peres could accurately say that "a close and fruitful working relationship between us evolved."[5]

Rabin presented his new government to the Knesset and the nation on July 13. With his wife and sister watching in the gallery, he delivered a direct and eloquent speech that left no doubt about how and where he intended to lead his country. "We are going to change the national order of priorities," he announced. While the prime minister mentioned dealing with unemployment, immigrant problems, and other social and economic issues, the government's "central goal" would be "to promote the making of peace and take vigorous steps that will lead to the end of the Arab-Israeli conflict." Rabin admitted to his people that the path he had chosen would involve "crises...disappointments, tears, and pain." But he reminded them that "this is a propitious hour, a time of great possibilities and opportunities" that Israel should not squander. "We do not intend to lose precious time," he said.

Then Rabin stopped talking to his people and in a remarkable and dramatic moment addressed their enemy and his, the Palestinians:

> *To you, the Palestinians in the territories, I wish to say from this rostrum: We have been fated to live together on this same patch of land, in the*

same country. We lead our lives with you, beside you and against you. You have failed in the war against us. One hundred years of your bloodshed and terror against us have brought you only suffering, humiliation, bereavement and pain. ...For forty-four years you have been living under a delusion. Your leaders have led you through lies and deceit. They have missed every opportunity, rejected all the proposals for a settlement, and have taken you from one tragedy to another.

To you, Palestinians who live in the territories...you who have never known a single day of freedom and joy in your lives—listen to us, if only this once. We offer you the fairest and most viable proposal from our standpoint today—autonomy, self-government—with all its advantages and limitations. You will not get everything you want. Perhaps neither will we. So once and for all, take your destiny in your own hands. Don't lose this opportunity that may never return. Take our proposal seriously—to avoid further suffering and grief; to end the shedding of tears and of blood.[6]

Rabin then turned back to his own people. He promised them that "when it comes to security, we will concede nothing," adding that "security takes preference even over peace." The new prime minister concluded by saying that his entire policy could be summed up from a single Biblical verse: "May the Lord give his people strength, may the Lord bless his people with peace...."[7] Nobody in the audience doubted that Israel would need all its strength to achieve the peace Rabin sought.

Working up to sixteen hours a day, Rabin moved quickly on several fronts. In July he visited Egyptian President Hosni Mubarak in Cairo. He announced a slow-down in housing construction on the West Bank, a move that pleased the United States. A visit to the United States and President George Bush improved the strained relations with Israel's main ally. During 1993, government spending on roads and other public facilities inside the 1967 borders both improved overall living conditions and stimulated the economy.

One of Rabin's most important long-term domestic efforts involved education, an area considered vital to Israel's future. The school day was lengthened. Over several years the education budget was increased by 50 percent. While there were sweeping changes in all areas of education, special attention was devoted to improving the teaching of science and technology. The results were impressive. In 1995 a delegation of educators from the United States said that their country should copy Israel's reforms in science education, while in 1996 a UN education expert said Israel may be the world leader in science education.

Of course, none of this brought peace any closer. During 1992, negotiations in Washington conducted under the Madrid framework made no progress. Meanwhile, Israel was rocked by a series of bloody attacks against both soldiers and civilians by Hamas and another Islamic fundamentalist organization opposed to any peace with Israel, called Hezbollah. The death toll mounted, but despite angry reactions from the political opposition and many Israeli citizens, Rabin refused to stop the peace negotiations. He knew that was exactly

*A Hamas suicide terrorist caused the destruction of
these buses resulting in the deaths of five people
and the injuries of more than one hundred. As
Rabin's peace negotiations continued, so did the deaths of
both Israeli soldiers and civilians as Hamas and Hezbollah
violently opposed any peace at all with Israel.*

what Hamas and Hezbollah wanted. As he told the people in a television interview:

> *Why has there been an increase in shooting incidents in recent months? I have no doubt that those who propose action are, first and foremost, the ones who want to kill...the peace and the chance to achieve peace.*[8]

Yet pressure was growing for Rabin to do something to increase the country's security. On December 16, after Hamas terrorists kidnapped and murdered a 29-year-old border policeman, the prime minister took action. Israeli forces rounded up 415 Hamas activists and other terrorist suspects and expelled them to Lebanon. It was not the first time that Israel had expelled Palestinian terrorist suspects, nor was the expulsion necessarily permanent. Those involved had the right to appeal their expulsion within sixty days. Nonetheless, the expulsion led to extensive international criticism of Israel. Rabin held out against pressures to revoke the expulsion. To his foreign critics he said that the murdered Israeli "was not granted the right to appeal the brutal, bloody sentence passed on him. The Hamas deportees do get that right."[9] Only after lengthy negotiations did Israel agree to allow the expelled men to return to their homes during the course of 1993.

In Israel, the expulsion shored up Rabin's reputation for toughness. So did his sealing off of the territories in March 1993, after a series of stabbings and attacks took fifteen Israeli lives in one month. The closure prevented would-be terrorists from reaching their intended victims. However, it also prevented other Palestinians, including 100,000 commuting to their jobs, from crossing into Israel. In July, after Hezbollah forces killed several Israeli soldiers and hit several northern Israeli towns with rockets, Rabin further demonstrated his willingness to use strong measures for security when the IDF bombarded southern Lebanon for a week. Eitan Haber, one of Rabin's closest aides and friends, summed up the rationale behind these measures: "If you want to make drastic concessions on peace, you must first show the public you can take drastic measures for security."[10]

Ironically, the peace negotiations at which concessions were being made were unknown to the Israeli public, and even to most members of Rabin's government. They had started in December 1992 and were taking place in secret in Oslo, Norway. These talks began as strictly unofficial discussions between private citizens. They were the latest example of unofficial contacts between Palestinians and Israelis that went back nearly twenty years. At times this secret "citizen diplomacy" involved contacts between Israelis and people connected with the PLO. Private meetings took place over the years despite an Israeli law, in effect from 1986 to January 1993, that prohibited Israelis from speaking to PLO officials and, far more menacing, the murder of several participating Palestinians by extremists within their own camp.

The so-called Oslo talks actually began in London before they were moved to Norway. The participants were several PLO officials and two Israeli academicians. However, what gave these talks special significance was the involvement behind the scenes of people in powerful positions within the PLO leadership and the Israeli government. On the Israeli side, the key link to the government was Yossi Beilin, Israel's deputy foreign minister and a long-time associate of Foreign Minister Shimon Peres. The stage manager for the PLO was a moderate member of its executive committee named Mahmoud Abbas (Abu Mazen), a veteran of many earlier attempts at "citizen diplomacy."

Critical support for the entire effort came from Norway, a country far from the Middle East but one with a long-standing concern with solving the Arab-Israeli conflict. A Norwegian academic named Terje Larsen, who was well connected to government officials, helped to get the talks started, while the Norwegian foreign ministry, headed by Johan Jorgen Holst, provided essential help in keeping the negotiations going.

Mahmoud Abbas described the Norwegian contribution to the talks:

> *It was a difficult task that required absolute secrecy....It imposed on the Israelis and Palestinians complete secrecy of movement, but also burdened the Norwegians with the even greater responsibility of controlling these movements on their territory in order not to attract the attention of foreign embassies, the media and the various intelligence services. It was an apparently impossible mission, but it was accomplished. The Norwegians continually moved the...negotiations from one place to another, so that no two consecutive meetings were held in the same place. They also restricted the number of people who would be responsible for the whole operation, who concealed themselves behind a wall of mist to prevent leaks to other Norwegian Foreign Ministry staff.[11]*

The talks, in fact, were so secret that Rabin himself initially did not know about them. The main architect of the Oslo talks from the Israeli side was Foreign Minister Shimon Peres. He told Beilin to pursue the idea and see what happened. The Israeli negotiators reported to Beilin, who in turn reported to Peres. When the talks, to almost everyone's surprise, seemed to be making progress, Peres went to Rabin early in February 1993. Rabin, cautious as ever, was reluctant at first to use what was called the Oslo "back channel." Apparently, Peres convinced him to support the talks by pointing out that they provided information on what the PLO was thinking without obligating the Israelis to anything.

Why did Rabin go along with this rather irregular diplomacy, and why with the PLO, whom he had repeatedly rejected as a negotiating partner? The answer lies in Rabin's speech to the Knesset, when he told his people that the world was changing quickly. It was "our duty," said Rabin, to "see the new world as it is now," being careful to "discern its dangers," but also making sure to "explore its prospects."[12] And there were new prospects, for several reasons.

The collapse of the Soviet Union had deprived the Arab forces most opposed to a peace with Israel of their main military backer. The PLO was weakened in addition by its support of Iraq during the Gulf War. This meant that Arafat might be ready to compromise before his organization weakened further. Meanwhile, the Intifada and the lack of progress under the Madrid framework had convinced Rabin that no other organization had any power to speak for the Palestinians. Rabin and Peres, therefore, concluded that if Israel wanted to reach an agreement with their adversaries, it had to be with the

PLO. They also recognized that given the rise of Islamic fundamentalism, if Israel did not deal with the PLO it soon might have no one left to deal with but Hamas, an organization utterly opposed to any peace with Israel.

In short, new conditions caused Rabin to change his mind about the PLO. It was not an easy decision. As a close advisor to Peres noted, to change Rabin needed "indisputable evidence that he is wrong. However, if there is a brick missing from the wall, he tears down the whole thing."[13] In this case, it appeared to Rabin that the bricks, slowly and one-by-one, were being put into place in Oslo. Throughout his career Rabin was above all a pragmatist and realist. Therefore, Peres recalled, once Rabin was convinced the Oslo negotiations *might* lead to peace, despite his continued doubts "he gave me, and the talks, a chance."[14]

Having decided to go ahead, Rabin worked closely with Peres. It was during their many long meetings that the two adversaries, both aging (Rabin, at seventy, was a year older than Peres) and aware that their time at center stage was running out, finally managed to overcome their personal antagonisms. In fact they had to, for they were working under extreme secrecy and almost alone. Probably no more than seven Israelis, including the negotiators, knew what was going on in Oslo.

The Oslo system of using private individuals rather than professional negotiators to represent Israel was not without its flaws. Early in the negotiations, the two Israeli academicians made concessions that were unacceptable to their government. In May, Rabin and Peres sent two government experts to Oslo to join the negotiating team. They had to make concessions on other less important issues in order to revise the unacceptable terms agreed to by the academicians.

The negotiations finally were completed in mid-August. On August 20, what was called the Declaration of Principles (DOP) was initialed by Peres representing Israel and Abbas representing the PLO. As Rabin had predicted in his Knesset speech thirteen months earlier, neither the Palestinians nor Israel got everything they wanted. He was well aware he had made significant and painful concessions to an organization he once had said that Israel could only meet on the battlefield.

The Oslo agreement called for Israel to withdraw its military forces from most of the Gaza Strip and the West bank city of Jericho and its environs by April 1994. What were called "authorized Palestinians" would then take over most local governmental functions, including police protection. In the future, the complicated document provided for self-rule to be extended to most of the rest of the West Bank. However, while Arabs would have self-rule under an elected Palestinian Council, Israel would continue to control foreign affairs and defense and have authority over Jewish settlements throughout the territories. Many complex issues—including the timing and pace of additional withdrawals, security arrangements, final borders, the Israeli settlements, and Jerusalem—were left for future negotiations over a five-year period.

When the Oslo accord was made public, a clear majority of Israelis supported it. Still, there was strong opposition from many quarters in Israeli society. Likud's new leader, Benjamin Netanyahu, the younger brother of "Yoni" Netanyahu, warned that the Oslo accord would lead to a Palestinian state and represented the "start of the destruction of Israel in line with the PLO plan."[15] Thousands of Jewish settlers from the West Bank and other Israelis who supported them demonstrated in protest. Rabin himself openly admitted that he had doubts. He told his Labor colleagues that he had no illusions about the PLO:

> *They killed. They are murderers, but peace you make with your enemies, including despicable enemies. I'm not going to beautify them. I can't tell you that some formulas in the agreement don't give me stomach pains. I have such pains, but I have to see also the comprehensive picture. We have to take risks.*[16]

On September 9, Yasir Arafat wrote a letter to Rabin in which he explicitly stated for the first time that the PLO recognized Israel's right to exist and accepted UN Resolutions 242 and 338. The next day, Prime Minister Rabin sent Arafat a letter recognizing the PLO. On September 13, both men, along with Peres and Abbas, stood on the White House lawn in Washington, D.C., with President Bill Clinton for an official signing of the Oslo accord. Rabin was proud of his role in reaching an agreement that could provide the basis for an Israeli-Palestinian peace. He knew that the picture of him shaking hands with Arafat was considered by people across the globe as a historic breakthrough.

Yet the White House ceremony and especially the handshake with Arafat were very difficult for Rabin. He could barely contain the personal loathing he felt for the PLO chairman. An Israeli reporter observed:

> *Rabin's body language seemed to communicate virtual physical pain. He twisted and turned constantly and the expression on his face—*

Rabin, President Clinton and Yasir Arafat pose for photographers prior to signing the peace accord agreed to in Oslo. The ceremony was difficult for Rabin, as he weighed the realization that he had negotiated with the PLO, which he'd sworn never to do, against the hope of security and peace for Israel.

particularly when he reached out to shake Arafat's
hand—remained an uncomfortable grimace
throughout the ceremony.[17]

As Rabin put it later, "Of all the hands in the world, it was not the hand I wanted or even dreamed of touching."[18] Yet he did so, because, as he told the small crowd on the White House lawn and the world watching on television, the time finally had come for "a new reckoning in the relations between peoples." In his short speech, Rabin quoted the timeless words from the Biblical book of Ecclesiastes:

> *To every thing there is a season and a time to every*
> *purpose under heaven. A time to be born and a*
> *time to die, a time to kill and a time to heal. A*
> *time to weep and a time to laugh. A time to love*
> *and a time to hate, a time of war and a time of*
> *peace.*

Then he added, "Ladies and gentlemen, the time for peace has come."[19]

When he returned home, Rabin had to defend the Oslo accord agreement in front of a divided Knesset, where even some Labor members had serious doubts about dealing with the PLO. Rabin rose to the occasion, telling his colleagues:

> *Members of the Knesset, we cannot choose our*
> *neighbors, or our enemies, not even the cruelest*
> *among them. We only have what there is. The*
> *PLO has fought against us, and we have fought*
> *against them—and with them we are today seeking*

*a path to peace.... We have the moral right not to
sit at the negotiating table with the PLO...not to
shake the hand that pulled the trigger. We have the
power to reject with revulsion the PLO proposals—
and then to be unwilling partners to the continuing cycle with which we have been forced to live
until now: war, terrorism, and violence.*[20]

After a heated debate the Knesset ratified the Oslo accord by a vote of 61 to 50, with nine members abstain-
ing. The governing body of the PLO did likewise.
Israeli-Palestinian relations were about to enter a new
and promising, but also difficult and dangerous, era.
Yitzhak Rabin personally was fated to do the same.

CHAPTER NINE

"I am not afraid."

The signing of the Oslo accord was only the beginning of what everyone involved knew would be a long and arduous peace process. Difficult negotiations lay ahead in order to resolve many thorny issues and implement the overall agreement. Rabin was well aware that the Oslo accord and future agreements would require Israel to make enormous concessions and take great risks. He also knew that he already had asked his people to accept conditions that he had emphatically rejected as recently as the election campaign of 1992. Not the least of them was the fact that he had negotiated with the PLO.

Rabin therefore knew it was crucial for the peace process that the PLO uphold its end of the bargain. Above all, Rabin and the Israeli public demanded an end to Palestinian terrorism that had taken so many lives. If the terrorism did not end, it would be extremely difficult for Rabin to get his people to go along with the peace process. Simply put, the peace process had to provide less violence and more peace.

During the following year the Oslo accord achieved nothing of the kind. In the last quarter of 1993 a wave of Hamas terror and murder left sixteen Israelis dead. Arafat and the PLO, who according to Oslo were supposed to represent and speak for the Palestinian people, seemed either unwilling or unable to control Hamas. The Israeli public reacted angrily. Support for the Oslo accord and for Rabin himself dropped noticeably.

On February 25, 1994, the peace process was nearly derailed by the mad act of an extremist Jewish settler from the town of Qiryat Arba near Hebron. Acting entirely on his own, the settler shot and killed 29 Muslims praying at the Tomb of the Patriarchs in Hebron, a site holy to both Jews and Muslims, and was himself beaten to death. Although Rabin and every leading Israeli politician denounced the crime in horror, the PLO suspended negotiations on implementing the Declaration of Principles (DOP) for a month.

Meanwhile, the Hamas-led wave of terror against Israel continued. By the end of 1994 the total number of bombing, shooting, and stabbing attacks exceeded 35. The worst occurred in October 1994 in Tel Aviv, when a suicide bomber blew himself up on a crowded morning rush-hour bus, killing 22 people and wounding 47. In January 1995, another suicide bomber killed 21 Israelis at a bus stop, most of them young soldiers. By then many Israelis agreed with President Ezer Weizman, a long-time advocate of peace negotiations, who said, "If the peace process is paved on the bodies of dead Jews, then I take it back."[1]

Nor did certain comments by Arafat help Rabin boost Israeli confidence in the peace process. In May 1994 a tape of Arafat speaking in a mosque became public. In his speech he called for a *jihad*—or holy war—for Jerusalem. Even more disconcerting, Arafat compared the Oslo accord to a truce that the prophet Mohammed had made with a Jewish tribe in Arabia early in the seventh century. From the start Mohammed considered the truce strictly a tactical maneuver until he could gain strength; he broke the truce ten years later and wiped out the Jewish tribe. Another serious problem for Rabin was the failure of Arafat and the PLO to honor their commitment to revise the PLO Covenant by eliminating the clauses calling for the destruction of Israel.

Rabin and Peres nonetheless held to their course. Echoing Ben-Gurion's words on the Yishuv's dual struggle with the British and the Nazis during World War II, Rabin said, "We shall fight the terror as if there were no peace talks, and we will conduct the peace talks as if there were no terror."[2]

Negotiations continued with the Palestinians on the specifics of the Israeli withdrawal from Gaza and Jericho. Rabin knew that despite support for the peace process, many Israelis remained skeptical and fearful. He was aware of the criticism that Peres and his dovish views played too large a role in the Oslo accord. He also was driven by his usual emphasis on security and the fact that he had more confidence in IDF officers than foreign ministry officials. Rabin therefore initially put top military officers in charge of the negotiations, although he later decided that Peres should lead the Israeli team. The result was an agreement completed in May 1994—five months behind schedule—more than 300 pages long (the

DOP was only 23 pages), filled with elaborate guarantees of military security even as Israel withdrew from Gaza and Jericho.

Rabin and Peres knew that in the wake of continued terrorist attacks they had to show results on several fronts to keep the peace process alive. October 1994 proved to be a good month for the Rabin-Peres team. The Nobel Prize selection committee in Oslo announced that the two men would share the 1994 Nobel Peace Prize with Arafat. (One of the committee's members resigned over the award to Arafat, citing the PLO leader's violent past.) Far more important, on October 26, Israel signed a peace treaty with Jordan. The treaty had been in the works for over a year, and was preceded by several preliminary agreements. Israel accepted a small change in the border in Jordan's favor and agreed to share more of the water from the Jordan and Yarmuk rivers with its eastern neighbor.

The actual signing of the peace treaty, in a dusty Jordanian border village just north of the Israeli town of Eilat and the Jordanian town of Aqaba, was a deeply emotional moment for both sides. It was not a gathering of strangers: Rabin, Peres, and other Israeli leaders had met with King Hussein many times over the years. In contrast to how he felt about Yasir Arafat, Rabin had both respect and genuine affection for Hussein. Rabin made this clear during his short speech when he addressed the king:

> *Your Majesty....I have learned to know and admire the quiet and the smiling power with which you guard your nation and the courage with which you lead your people. It is not*

*only...our states that are making peace with
each other today, not only our nations that are
shaking hands in peace here....You and I, Your
Majesty, are making peace here, our own peace,
the peace of soldiers and the peace of friends.³*

Hussein expressed similar sentiments, both for Rabin
and other Israeli leaders present such as Peres and
Weizman, men he referred to as "colleagues and friends."
The Jordanian king stressed that he envisioned the type
of genuine peace that Israelis wanted to see. It would not
be like the disappointing "Cold Peace" with Egypt, which
the Egyptians had kept strictly limited to a formal relationship between governments with little contact between
Egyptians and Israelis. Instead, said Hussein:

*This is a peace of dignity. This is peace with
commitment. This is our gift to our peoples
and the generations to come. It will herald the
change in the quality of life of people. It will
not simply be a piece of paper ratified by those
responsible, blessed by the world. It will be real,
as we open our hearts and minds to each other,
as we discover a human face to everything that
has happened and to each other—for all of us
have suffered for too long.⁴*

Virtually all Israelis agreed that the Jordanian treaty held
great promise at an acceptable risk. Netanyahu and the
Likud lined up behind the agreement. It passed the
Knesset by an overwhelming vote of 105 to 3, with 6
abstentions. It was not easy to recall any issue that so
united that generally contentious body.

Nevertheless, it did not take long until bitter divisions again plagued the peace process, especially as the terror continued and more Israelis died. By April 1995, less than half of all Israelis favored the peace process, and more supported Netanyahu for prime minister than supported Rabin. The language of Israeli politics, never restrained and sometimes unacceptably strident by American standards, grew increasingly heated. Those for and against the peace process hurled insults at each other, both from political platforms and in the streets. It seemed to many that the "peace process" was beginning to tear Israel apart.

Some of those who disagreed with Rabin came from the ranks of his own Labor party. They formed a new organization called The Third Way. This group—it was not a political party positioned itself between Likud, which opposed all territorial concessions, and Labor, which clearly was preparing for extensive concessions in the West Bank and possibly a complete return of the Golan Heights to Syria in return for a peace treaty. (Israel was negotiating separately with Syria as well as with the PLO.) The Third Way was headed by Avigdor Kahalani, a Labor member of parliament and a military hero in both the Six-Day and Yom Kippur wars. Another leader was Dan Shomron, the overall commander at Entebbe and a former IDF chief of staff.

Still, negotiations with the PLO continued, this time with the goal of extending the Gaza-Jericho agreement and Palestinian self-rule to much of the West Bank. The terror bombings also continued, killing ten Israelis in two bus attacks in July and August. Finally, an agreement that has become known as Oslo II was reached. Its official signing took place on the White House lawn on September 28, 1995. Oslo II initially divided the West Bank into three zones. Area "A", about 3 percent of the land, included the region's major urban areas, where the Palestinians would be given full territorial and security control during late 1995 and early 1996. Area "B" included about 465 Palestinian villages and 27 percent of the land. Here Israel would turn over partial control to the Palestinians during 1996, but retain control of military security. The remainder of the West Bank (Area "C") would remain under Israeli control until a final settlement was reached. It included all the Israeli settlements and the uninhabited parts of the region, including the Jordan River valley.

Oslo II met with stiff opposition in Israel. The Knesset staged a marathon fifteen-hour debate, during which more than 100 of its 120 members spoke. Rabin vigorously defended the agreement, stressing its security arrangements. He also pointed out that Israel, a democratic society, could not continue to rule the large Arab population of the West Bank and Gaya:

> *We had to choose between a Greater Land of Israel, which means a binational state and whose population would comprise, as of today, 4.5 million Jews and more than 3 million Palestinians, which are a separate entity— religious, political and national—and a state smaller in area, but which would be a Jewish state. We chose a Jewish state.*[5]

Tempers flared, as Rabin, Netanyahu, and others angrily attacked each other. Critics said the agreement was paving the way for Israel's return virtually to its insecure

1967 borders and the creation of a Palestinian state. In the end, the Knesset approved Oslo II by the narrowest possible margin, 61 to 59. Among those voting no were Kahalani and another Labor member of The Third Way. Rabin's critics were quick to point out that 5 of his 61 votes came from Arab members of the Knesset. Among the Knesset's Jewish delegates, only 56 voted for Oslo II, while 59 voted against. Meanwhile, public-opinion polls showed continued confusion and doubt: support for the peace process but also a lack of confidence in the agreements reached with the PLO.

In the aftermath of the Oslo II vote, Israel's political atmosphere grew even more stormy. In many ways the angry divisions were reminiscent of what Rabin had seen and lamented as ambassador to the United States during the Vietnam War. About a week after the vote, he was invited to speak at a gathering of immigrants from English-speaking countries. Some people in the crowd shouted him down. Rabin was furious and told the crowd so. Meanwhile, at antigovernment rallies some angry protesters called Rabin a traitor. Concern spread among politicians on both sides that matters were getting out of hand. On several occasions Netanyahu criticized anti-Rabin protesters for going too far. "We'll win by the vote, not by violence," he told one crowd.[6] In the Labor camp, Rabin's advisors feared for his safety, but he refused to take precautions such as wearing a bulletproof vest. "I am not afraid personally," he said. "I will not run away and let them silence me."[7]

Like every democracy, Israel has its seething and hostile political fringe where fanatical people scheme to silence those with whom they disagree. In 1963 in the United States a fanatic assassinated President John F.

Kennedy; in 1968, Rabin's first year as ambassador, fanatics took the lives of Martin Luther King, Jr., and Senator Robert F. Kennedy. In Israel, small groups of Jewish extremist West Bank settlers and their supporters belonged to that violent fringe. In February 1994 one of them murdered the Arab worshippers in Hebron, an act that horrified virtually all Israelis. On November 4, 1995, another fanatic struck, this time against Prime Minister Yitzhak Rabin.

Rabin was assassinated at a huge rally organized by the Labor party to counter opposition rallies and to demonstrate support for the peace process. More than 100,000 people gathered in Tel Aviv's Kings of Israel Square to cheer for Rabin and Peres and their policies. It was an extraordinary event. Normally ill at ease in public, Rabin on this day was relaxed and clearly enjoying himself. Revitalized by a sense that the country indeed supported him, Rabin spoke passionately to the crowd. "This government, which I have the privilege to head with my friend Shimon Peres, decided to give peace a chance," he said.[8] After his speech, Rabin joined with his audience in singing the "Song of Peace," a hit from the 1970s that over the years had become one of the most popular songs in Israel. Then, standing on the platform with Peres, he put his arm around his old rival, who after decades of feuding he finally could call "my friend," and greeted well-wishers.

When the time came to leave, Rabin walked to a waiting car. A young Jewish law student named Yigal Amir waited in the shadows. Amir held extreme religious views; he later told police that he had "received instructions from God to kill Prime Minister Rabin."[9] After months of stalking the prime minister, Amir finally

Speaking at the giant peace demonstration on November 4, 1995, one hour before an assassin's bullet would take his life.

had slipped through the tight security net that surrounded his prey. It was 9:40 P.M. Shots rang out. One of Rabin's bodyguards immediately threw himself on the prime minister, stopping one of the bullets with his own body. Within seconds Rabin was in the car and within two minutes in a hospital. But it was too late. The two bullets that hit the prime minister did massive damage. Desperate efforts by doctors to save him failed. Yitzhak Rabin, who had survived so many battles, was dead.

The assassination stunned Israel and much of the world. Israeli life came to a stop. An entire nation stood as if in a daze. People hardly knew what to think or say. The nation mourned, both for its fallen leader and for itself. In this small country, under siege for its entire history, where all young people answered the call of national defense and no family could escape the pain of war and terror, people were used to mourning together, as a family, when others lost a loved one to enemy fire or bombs. Where else did national leaders regularly attend the funerals of fallen soldiers or victims of terror? Yet something had gone terribly wrong. The intensity of the debate had flared out of control and created an atmosphere of anger and intolerance in which extremists could unleash their fury. Over the years Israelis, and especially their politicians, certainly had their differences, but who could have believed that the divisions and anger would come to this?

On November 5, a million people, nearly one Israeli in five, filed past Rabin's simple pine coffin at the Knesset. Rabin was buried on Monday, November 6. Leaders from more than eighty countries attended the funeral. Yasir Arafat asked to attend, but was not permitted for security reasons. The ceremony was carried live

Rabin's assassination provoked deep anguish in people around the world. Here an Arab man cries at a roadside memorial.

on television in countries throughout the world. Israeli and foreign leaders spoke of Rabin with deep respect and affection. Shimon Peres, speaking for "a nation with tears in their eyes," grieved the loss of the "youngest among Israel's generals...the greatest of Israel's peace-makers" and a man he called "my eldest brother." King Hussein mourned "a brother, a colleague and friend" who "lived as a soldier and died as a soldier for peace." President Bill Clinton told the Israeli people that he joined them in mourning the loss of "my partner and friend." The American president added that "Israel's covenant with God—for freedom, for tolerance, for security for peace—that covenant must hold. That covenant was Prime Minister Rabin's life work, now we must make it his lasting legacy."[10]

The most moving eulogy came not from a world leader but from seventeen-year-old Noa Ben-Artzi Filosof, Yitzhak Rabin's granddaughter. Her freckled face and reddish-brown hair, as well as her self-control, could not help but evoke memories of a young Yitzhak Rabin. Noa apologized for not wanting to talk about peace; she wanted to talk about her *saba*, her grandfather. She recalled "the caresses of your warm soft hands...your warm embrace that was reserved only for us...your half smile that always told me so much, that same smile which is no longer." Struggling to hold back tears, she concluded: "I imagine angels are accompanying you now and I ask them to take care of you, because you deserve their protection."[11]

When Israel lost Yitzhak Rabin, it lost a soldier and a statesman. It lost a military hero who knew how to prepare for and fight wars, and who did so brilliantly. It lost a political leader who understood that no war is com-

Rabin's granddaughter, Noa Ben-Artzi Filosof, weeps as she delivers the eulogy not for Rabin the statesman and soldier, but for Yitzhak Rabin, her grandfather.

pletely won unless the victory leads to peace. It lost a patriot who when waging war or making peace was guided by a stern and consistent realism, an outlook that demanded caution in preparing for battles or negotiations but sanctioned taking risks when the situation demanded. It lost a prime minister prepared to make the hard decisions, capable of adjusting to new conditions, and fortified with the inner strength to see things through. And it lost a visionary who did not let his dream for peace make him lose sight of the reality that Israel always had to protect its security.

When Yitzhak Rabin died he was at the center of an emotional public debate. His popularity had declined since 1992, and it was not at all certain that he and Labor would win the upcoming elections in 1996. Israelis of goodwill and common sense who wanted peace could be found on both sides of the debate over the peace process, with strong arguments to support their positions. But despite Israel's divisions and disagreements, Rabin was convinced that he had compelling reasons to continue his policies. As he told the crowd in Tel Aviv only ninety minutes before his assassination:

> *I was a military man for twenty-seven years. I waged war as long as there was no chance for peace. I believe there is now a chance for peace, a great chance, and we must take advantage of it.*[12]

That job has now fallen to his successors.

CHRONOLOGY

1920   Nehemiah Rabin meets Rosa Cohen in Jerusalem after each rushes to the Old City to help protect local Jews under attack from Arab rioters.

1921   Rabin and Cohen are married.

1922   March 1: Yitzhak Rabin is born in Jerusalem.

1936   Arab Revolt in Palestine begins.

1937   October: Rabin enters the Kadoorie Agricultural High School.

           November: Rosa Cohen dies from heart disease.

1939   September: World War II begins.

1940	Rabin graduates from high school; declines opportunity to study water engineering at the University of California at Berkeley.
1941	Rabin joins the Palmach and takes part in sabotage mission in Lebanon.
1943	Rabin is promoted to platoon leader.
1944	Rabin meets Leah Schlossberg.
1945	May: World War II ends. The full extent of the Nazi genocide against the Jews becomes known. The Yishuv smuggles Jewish refugees into Palestine in defiance of the British.
	October: Rabin helps lead the Atlit raid.
1946	June: Rabin is arrested along with other Hagana activists, including his father. They are held until November.
	November: Rabin decides once again not to attend Berkeley. He takes command of the Palmach's Second Battalion instead.
1947	February: Britain decides to give up its mandate and leave Palestine.
	October: Yigal Allon appoints Rabin deputy commander of the Palmach.
	November 19: The UN General Assembly votes to divide Palestine into a Jewish state and an Arab state. The Jews accept the decision; the Arabs reject it. Arabs begin attacking Jews throughout Palestine.

1948	April: The Harel Brigade under Rabin's command fights to keep open the road to Jerusalem and defend the Jewish Quarter in the Old City. The battle continues into May.
	May 14: Israel officially declares its independence.
	May 15: Five Arab armies invade Israel. The War of Independence officially begins.
	May 28: The Jewish Quarter falls to the Arab Legion. Rabin watches the surrender take place from just outside the Old City walls.
	June-July: Israeli resistance stiffens, and the tide of battle turns in Israel's favor.
	August 23: Yitzhak Rabin and Leah Schlossberg are married.
	October-December: Israeli forces on the southern front, where Allon is commander and Rabin is deputy commander, win major victories.
1949	January: Armistice talks begin on Rhodes. Rabin is part of the Israeli delegation.
	February: Armistice agreement is signed.
	March: Israel is admitted to the United Nations.
1950	The Rabins' daughter, Dalia, is born. A son, Yuval, is born in 1955.
1951	Rabin becomes head of the IDF operations division. He is now on the IDF's general staff.

1952	The Rabins move to Zahala
1952-1953	Rabin studies at the British army's Royal Staff College in Camberley, England.
1954	Rabin is promoted to rank of major-general.
1956	Rabin is appointed commander of the Northern Command.
	October-November: The Sinai Campaign. Israel overruns the Gaza Strip and the Sinai Peninsula.
1957	Israel withdraws from Sinai. A UN peace-keeping force is positioned in the Sinai.
1959	Rabin becomes the IDF's second-ranking officer after a shake-up of its top command.
1964	January 1: Rabin becomes the IDF Chief of Staff.
	May: Palestine Liberation Organization is formed.
1965	The IDF destroys the Syrian project to divert tributaries of the Jordan River.
1966	Prime Minister Eshkol asks Rabin to serve another year as chief of staff.
1967	May: Egypt sends troops into the Sinai Peninsula. UN peace-keeping troops withdraw. Egypt blockades the Straits of Tiran. Arab troops mass along Israel's borders.

May 23–24: Rabin suffers from nervous exhaustion. He returns to work on May 25.

June 5: Israel attacks Egyptian airfields. The Six-Day War begins.

June 7: Israeli troops take the Old City and the Western Wall.

June 10: The Six-Day War ends. Israel controls the West Bank, the Gaza Strip, all of Jerusalem, and the Golan Heights.

November 22: The UN Security Council passes Resolution 242.

1968   March: Rabin begins his tour of duty as Israel's ambassador to the United States. He serves in that post until 1973.

1969   Golda Meir becomes prime minister.

1969-1970   The War of Attrition along the Suez Canal.

1970   September: "Black September" in Jordan. Israel responds to American request to aid Jordan in the face of Syrian tank incursion.

September 28: Gamal Abdel Nasser dies. He is succeeded as president of Egypt by Anwar Sadat.

1972   September: PLO terrorists murder eleven Israeli athletes at the Olympic Games at Munich.

1973   Rabin returns to Israel and enters politics as member of the Labor party.

October 6: Egypt and Syria attack Israel. The Yom Kippur War begins. Israel defeats the invaders but suffers very high casualties.

December: Labor wins elections. Rabin becomes minister of labor in Golda Meir's new cabinet.

1974   April: Meir and Defense Minister Moshe Dayan resign after public criticism of their failure to prepare Israel for war. Rabin defeats Shimon Peres for the post of leader of the Labor party.

June 3: Prime Minister Rabin presents his government to the Knesset. Peres becomes defense minister. The two men feud throughout Rabin's tenure as prime minister.

1975   April: PLO terrorists murder eighteen people in Kiryat Shmona.

May: PLO terrorist attack leaves twenty children dead in Ma'alot.

September: After long and tedious negotiations conducted by U.S. Secretary of State Henry Kissinger, a separation of forces agreement is reached between Israel and Egypt involving significant Israeli withdrawals in the Sinai.

1976   June–July: Arab and German terrorists hijack an Air France jet with many Israeli passengers to Entebbe, Uganda. The hostages are rescued in a daring raid mounted by the IDF.

1977	March: Scandal of Leah Rabin's U.S. bank account leads to Rabin's resignation as prime minister.
	May: Likud defeats labor in national elections. Menachem Begin becomes prime minister.
1977–1984	Rabin is an opposition member of the Knesset.
1977	November: Sadat comes to Jerusalem.
1978	September: Camp David Accords are signed.
1979	March: Israeli-Egyptian peace treaty is signed. The agreement with Egypt turns out to be a "Cold Peace."
1980	December: Peres defeats Rabin for post of Labor party leader.
1981	June: Israel bombs and destroys Iraq's nuclear reactor.
1982	June: Israel invades Lebanon to drive the PLO from the southern part of the country, but becomes bogged down there.
1983	August: Begin suddenly retires and is replaced as prime minister by Yitzhak Shamir.
1984	September: National Unity government is formed after deadlocked election. Rabin is named minister of defense.

1987	December: The Intifada begins. Rabin responds with "iron fist" policy, but cannot stop the uprising.
1988	November: Another dead-heat election. Unity government continues with Rabin still minister of defense.
1990	March: Labor quits the unity government. July: Peres again defeats Rabin for Labor party leadership.
1991	January: The Gulf War. United States-led coalition drives Iraqi forces from Kuwait. Israel is attacked by Iraqi Scud missiles but agrees not to respond to the attack. October: Madrid peace conference opens.
1992	February: Rabin defeats Peres for Labor party leadership. June: Labor defeats Likud in national elections. July: Rabin again becomes prime minister. Peres is foreign minister in the new Labor government. December: Israel deports more than 400 Hamas activists to Lebanon. December: Secret talks between Israelis and representatives of the PLO begin in London. They continue in Oslo, Norway.

1993	February: Rabin is informed of the Oslo talks and decides to pursue them.
	March: Rabin seals off the West Bank and Gaza.
	July: The IDF bombards Lebanon.
	August: Oslo negotiations are completed, and a Declaration of Principles (DOP) is signed.
	September 9–10: PLO recognizes Israel's right to exist and UN Resolution 242. Israel recognizes PLO.
	September 13: Formal signing of DOP at the White House. Rabin and Arafat shake hands.
	October: Knesset ratifies the Oslo accord.
1994	May: Agreement is reached on the details of Israel's withdrawal from Gaza and Jericho.
	October: Announcement that Rabin, Peres, and Arafat will share the 1994 Nobel Peace Prize.
	October 26: Peace treaty signed with Jordan.
1995	Hamas terrorist attacks continue to take many Israeli lives. Israel is deeply divided over the peace process.
	September 28: Oslo II, which extends Palestinian self-rule to much of the West Bank, is signed at the White House.

1995	October: After heated debate, the Knesset approvés Oslo II by a vote of 61 to 59. A majority of Jewish members of the Knesset oppose the agreement.
	October: Rabin is heckled while trying to address a gathering of English-speaking immigrants.
	November 4: Yitzhak Rabin is assassinated after speaking at a huge and enthusiastic peace rally in Tel Aviv.

NOTES

Chapter One

1. Yitzhak Rabin, *The Rabin Memoirs* (Boston: Little, Brown, 1979), p. 15.
2. Ibid.
3. Ibid. p. 16.
4. Ibid.
5. Ibid.
6. Ibid. p. 17.
7. Quoted in Robert Slater, *Rabin of Israel* (New York: St. Martin's Press, 1993), p. 57.

Chapter Two

1. *The Rabin Memoirs,* p. 3.
2. Ibid. p. 5.
3. Quoted in Abba Eban, *My Country: The Story of Modern Israel* (New York: Random House, 1972), p. 10.

4. *The Rabin Memoirs*, p. 6.
5. Ibid.
6. Quoted in Slater, *Rabin of Israel*, p. 28.
7. *The Rabin Memoirs*, p. 6.
8. Quoted in Slater, p. 29.
9. *The Rabin Memoirs*, p. 6.
10. Quoted in Slater, p. 41.
11. Quoted in Slater, p. 43.
12. Quoted in Conner Cruise O'Brien, *The Siege: The Story of Israel and Zionism* (London: Paladin, 1986), p. 233.
13. Quoted in O'Brien, pp. 242–243.
14. ABC News Documentary, "Rabin: Action Biography," April 15, 1975.
15. *The Rabin Memoirs*, pp. 11–12.
16. Ibid. p. 13
17. Ibid.
18. Ibid. p. 35.
19. Quoted in Slater, p. 51.
20. *The Rabin Memoirs*, p. 35.

Chapter Three

1. Quoted in Howard M. Sachar, *A History of Israel: From the Rise of Zionism to Our Time* (New York: Knopf, 1976), p. 270.
2. *The Rabin Memoirs*, p. 17.
3. Ibid. p. 19.
4. Quoted in Eban, *My Country: The Story of Modern Israel*, p. 48.
5. *The Rabin Memoirs*, p. 19.
6. Quoted in Eban, p. 9.
7. *The Rabin Memoirs*, p. 29.
8. Quoted in Eban, p. 12.
9. Quoted in Sachar, p. 297.
10. *The Rabin Memoirs*, p. 32.

11. Quoted in Eban, p. 57.
12. *The Rabin Memoirs*, p. 36.
13. Quoted in Slater, *Rabin of Israel: Warrior for Peace*, p. 82.
14. *The Rabin Memoirs*, p. 42.

Chapter Four

1. *Al-Misri*, April 12, 1954. (An Egyptian newspaper)
2. *The Rabin Memoirs*, p. 45.
3. Quoted in Slater, *Rabin of Israel: Warrior for Peace*, p. 104.
4. *Middle East Affairs*, December 1956, p. 461.
5. *The Rabin Memoirs*, p. 52.
6. Ibid. p. 62.
7. Ibid. p. 63.
8. Quoted in Slater, p. 112.
9. *The Rabin Memoirs*, p. 68.
10. Quoted in Sachar, *A History of Israel*, p. 616.
11. Quoted in Slater, p. 125.
12. *The Rabin Memoirs*, p. 81.
13. Ibid. p. 81.
14. Quoted in Slater, p. 130.
15. Quoted in *The Rabin Memoirs*, p. 87.
16. Quoted in Ian Black and Benny Morris, *Israel's Secret Wars: A History of Israel's Intelligence* (London: Futura, 1991), p. 220.
17. Ibid.
18. Quoted in Sachar, p. 633.
19. Quoted in Eban, p. 214.
20. Quoted in Nadav Safran, *From War to War: The Arab-Israeli Confrontation, 1948–1967* (New York: Pegasus, 1969), p. 324.
21. *The Rabin Memoirs*, p. 104.
22. Quoted in Slater, p. 139.

23. Quoted in Safran, p. 348.
24. Quoted in *The Rabin Memoirs*, p. 108.
25. *The Rabin Memoirs*, pp. 111–112.
26. Quoted in *The Rabin Memoirs*, p. 115.
27. Quoted in Slater, pp. 148–149.

Chapter Five

1. Quoted in *The Rabin Memoirs*, p. 122.
2. Quoted in Sachar, *A History of Israel*, p. 673.
3. Ibid.
4. "Resolutions of the Khartoum Conference," in Ian J. Bickerton and Carla L. Klausner, *A Concise History of the Arab-Israeli Conflict*, 2nd ed. (Englewood Cliffs, NJ: Prentice Hall, 1995), p. 157.
5. *The Rabin Memoirs*, p. 125.
6. Ibid. pp. 127–128.
7. Quoted in Slater, *Rabine of Israel*, p. 188.
8. Quoted in Yossi Melman and Dan Raviv, *Friends in Deed: Inside the U.S.-Israeli Alliance* (New York: Hyperion, 1994), p. 157.
9. *The Rabin Memoirs*, p. 231.
10. Henry Kissinger, *White House Years* (Boston: Little, Brown, 1979), p. 355.
11. *The Rabin Memoirs*, p. 169.
12. Ibid. p. 198.
13. Ibid. pp. 226–227.
14. Ibid. p. 232.
15. Quoted in Slater, p. 189.

Chapter Six

1. Quoted in Sachar, *A History of Israel*, p. 740.
2. Golda Meir, *My Life* (London: Weidenfeld and Nicolson, 1975), p. 359.

3. *The Rabin Memoirs*, pp. 235–236.
4. Quoted in Chaim Herzog, *The War of Atonement: October 1973* (Boston: Little, Brown, 1975), p. 113.
5. *The Rabin Memoirs*, p. 236.
6. Ibid. p. 238.
7. Shimon Peres, *Battling for Peace: A Memoir*, edited by David Landau (New York: Random House, 1995), p. 144.
8. Ibid. p. 240.
9. Ibid. p. 241
10. Quoted in Slater, *Rabin of Israel*, p. 219.
11. *The Rabin Memoirs*. p. 242.
12. Ibid. p. 247.
13. Quoted in Slater, p. 237.
14. *The Rabin Memoirs*, p. 256.
15. Quoted in Howard Sachar, *A History of Israel: Volume II, From the Aftermath of the Yom Kippur War* (New York and Oxford: Oxford University Press, 1987), p. 7.
16. Quoted in William Stevenson, *90 Minutes to Entebbe* (New York: Bantam Books, 1976), pp. 82–83.
17. Quoted in Slater, p. 252.
18. Quoted in Stevenson, pp. 121–122.
19. *The Rabin Memoirs*, p. 288.
20. Quoted in Sachar, *A History of Israel*, vol. II, p. 19.

Chapter Seven

1. Quoted in Slater, *Rabin of Israel*, p. 299.
2. Quoted in O'Connor, p. 574.
3. *The Rabin Memoirs*, pp. 322-323.
4. Ibid. p. 324.
5. Ibid. p. 329.
6. Quoted in Sachar, *A History of Israel*, vol. II, p. 127.
7. Quoted in Slater, p. 318.
8. Quoted in Slater, p. 325.

9. *Time*, February 2, 1985.
10. Quoted in Slater, p. 340.
11. Quoted in Ze'ev Schiff and Ehud Ya'ari, *Intifada: The Inside Story of the Uprising That Changed the Middle East Equation* (New York: Simon & Schuster, 1989), p.144.
12. Quoted in Slater, p. 342.
13. Quoted in Bickerton and Klausner, *A Concise History of the Arab-Israeli Conflict*, p. 229.

Chapter Eight

1. Quoted in Slater, *Rabin of Israel*, p. 377.
2. Quoted in Gideon Doron, "Labor's Return to Power in Israel." *Current History*, January 1993, p. 30.
3. *The Jerusalem Post*, June 1, 1992.
4. Quoted in Slater, p. 401.
5. *Battling for Peace*, p. 272.
6. Quoted in the preface to *The Rabin Memoirs*, 2nd ed. (Bnei Brak, Israel: Steimatsky Ltd., 1994), pp. v–vi.
7. Ibid. p. 9.
8. Quoted in Slater, p. 446.
9. Quoted in Slater, p. 448.
10. Quoted in David Makovsky, *Making Peace With the PLO: The Rabin Government's Road to the Oslo Accord* (Boulder, CO: Westview Press, 1996), p. 87.
11. Mahmoud Abbas (Abu Mazen), *Through Secret Channels*, pp. 103–104.
12. Quoted in *The Rabin Memoirs*, 2nd ed., p. v.
13. Quoted in Makovsky, p. 119.
14. *Battling for Peace*, p. 285.
15. Quoted in Bickerton and Klausner, p. 269.
16. Quoted in Robert Slater, *Rabin of Israel: Warrior for Peace* (New York: HarperCollins, 1996), p. 583. Note that all other Slater citations refer to 1993 edition cited in Chapter One, note 7.

17. Makovsky, p. 81.

18. *Time*, November 13, 1995, p. 71.

19. "Rabin Statement at Signing of Accord," in Bickerton and Klausner, p. 283.

20. Quoted in Howard M. Sachar, *A History of Israel From the Rise of Zionism to Our Time*, 2nd ed., revised and updated (New York: Knopf, 1996), p. 993.

Chapter Nine

1. Quoted in Slater, *Rabin of Israel*, p. 599.

2. Quoted in Slater, p. 588.

3. *The New York Times*, October 27, 1994, p. A12.

4. Ibid.

5. *The Jerusalem Post International Edition*, October 14, 1995, p. 2.

6. *The Jerusalem Post International Edition*, October 21, 1995, p. 4.

7. Ibid.

8. *The Jerusalem Post International Edition*, November 11, 1995, p. 3.

9. Ibid. p. 2.

10. *The New York Times*, November 7, 1995, p. A10.

11. Ibid. p. A11.

12. *The Jerusalem Post International Edition*, November 11, 1995, p. 3.

BIBLIOGRAPHY

Abbas, Mahmoud (Abu Mazen). *Through Secret Channels.* Reading, England: Garnett, 1995.

Bickerton, Ian J. and Carla L. Klausner. *A Concise History of the Arab-Israeli Conflict,* 2nd ed. Englewood Cliffs, NJ: Prentice Hall, 1995.

Black, Ian and Benny Morris. *Israel's Secret Wars: A History of Israel's Secret Services.* London: Futura, 1991.

Freedman, Robert O., editor. *Israel Under Rabin.* Boulder, CO: Westview, 1995.

Golan, Matti. *Shimon Peres.* New York: St. Martin's Press, 1982.

Herzog, Chaim. *The War of Atonement: October, 1973.* Boston: Little, Brown, 1975.

Katz, Samuel M. *Soldier Spies: Israeli Military Intelligence.* Novato, CA: Presidio, 1992.

Laqueur, Walter and Barry Rubin, editors. *The Israel-Arab Reader: A Documentary History of the Middle East Conflict,* 5th revised and updated edition. New York and London: Penguin, 1995.

Livingstone Neil C. and David Halevy. *Inside the PLO.* New York: William Morrow, 1990.

Makovsky, David. *Making Peace With the PLO: The Rabin Government's Road to the Oslo Accord.* Boulder, CO: Westview, 1996.

Melman, Yossi and Dan Raviv. *Friends in Deed: Inside the U.S.-Israel Alliance.* New York: Hyperion, 1994.

O'Brien, Conor Cruise. *The Siege: The Story of Israel and Zionism.* London: Paladin, 1988.

Peres, Shimon. *Battling for Peace: A Memoir.* New York: Random House, 1995.

Perlmutter, Amos. *Israel: The Partitioned State: A Political History Since 1900.* New York: Charles Scribner's Sons, 1985.

Rabin, Yitzhak. *The Rabin Memoirs.* Boston: Little, Brown, 1979.

Sachar, Howard M. *A History of Israel From the Rise of Zionism to Our Time.* New York: Knopf, 1976.

Sachar, Howard M. *A History of Israel: Volume II, From the Aftermath of the Yom Kippur War.* New York and Oxford: Oxford University Press, 1987.

Safran, Nadav. *From War to War: The Arab-Israeli Confrontation, 1948-1967.* New York: Pegasus, 1969.

Schiff, Ze'ev and Ehud Ya'ari. *Intifada: The Inside Story of the Palestinian Uprising That Changed the Middle East Equation.* New York: Simon & Schuster, 1989.

Slater, Robert. *Rabin of Israel.* New York: St. Martin's Press, 1993.

Stevenson, William. *90 Minutes at Entebbe.* New York: Bantam, 1976.

INDEX

Kennedy, John F., 155-156

Kennedy, Robert F., 84, 156

Kibbutz Bet Oren, 14, 15

Kibbutz Yagur, 12, 14, 15

King, Martin Luther, Jr., 82, 156

Kiryat Arba, 110

Kiryat Shmona, 100

Kissinger, Henry, 85, *86*, 87, 89, 99, 102

Knesset, 94, 99, 114, 115, 152, 154, 155

Kuwait, 118, 127

Labor party, 39, 94-95, 98, 99, 108, 117, 118, 120, 125-127, 129-133, 153, 156, 162

Lake Kinneret (Sea of Galilee), 21, 43, 63, 64, 132

Larsen, Terje, 140

Latrun fortress, 47

League of Nations, 19

Lebanon, 31, 32, 45, 88, 119-121, 128, 139

Lehi, 38, 42

Levy, David, 131

Libya, 42

Likud party, 39, 94, 109, 110, 112, 113, 117-120, 123, 125, 126, 129-133, 152, 153

Lydda, 46

Ma'alot, 101

Madrid Conference, 127-128

Mandate system, 19-20

McGovern, George, 92

Meany, George, 91

Meir, Golda, 22, 47, 85, 95-96, 98

Mitla pass, 102, 103

Mohammed, 150

Mount Carmel, 14

Mubarak, Hosni, 136

Munich Olympic Games (1970), 81

Muslims, 17, 18

Narkiss, Uzi, 72, *73*, 79

Nasser, Gamal Abdel, 60, 66, 67, 69, 90

Nazareth, 48

Negev desert, 42, 48, 50, 52

Netanyahu, Benjamin, 143, 152-155

Netanyahu, Yonatan, 106-108

Nixon, Richard, 84, 85, 92, 101